" *Good fences make good neighbors.*"

Robert Frost, *Mending Wall*

A view of one of the many authentic fences and gardens in Old Salem.
Old Salem is a living history town in Winston Salem, NC.

BUILDING
FENCES + GATES

BUILDING FENCES + GATES

HOW TO DESIGN AND BUILD THEM FROM THE GROUND UP

Richard Freudenberger   **Photography Richard Babb**

Lark Books

Asheville, North Carolina

Art Director: Dana Irwin
Illustrations: Olivier Rollin
Production: Dana Irwin, Bobby Gold

Library of Congress Cataloging-in-Publication Data Available
Freudenberger, Richard .

     Building fences + gates : how to design and build them from the ground up /
     Richard Freudenberger. — 1st ed.
     p.   cm.
     Includes index.
     ISBN 1-57990-046-1 — 1-887374-47-7 (pbk)
     1. Fences—Design and construction—Amateurs' manuals. 2. Gates—Design and construction—Amateurs' manuals.
I. Title
TH4965.F74   1997
631.2'7—dc21   97-24675
                                            CIP

10 9 8 7 6 5 4 3 2 1

First Edition

Published by Lark Books
50 College St.
Asheville, NC 28801, USA

© 1997, Altamont Press

Distributed by Random House, Inc., in the United States, Canada,
    the United Kingdom, Europe, and Asia

Distributed in Australia by Capricorn Link (Australia) Pty Ltd.,
    P.O. Box 6651, Baulkham Hills Business Centre, NSW 2153,
    Australia

Distributed in New Zealand by Tandem Press Ltd., 2 Rugby Rd.,
    Birkenhead, Auckland, New Zealand

Printed in Hong Kong

CONTENTS

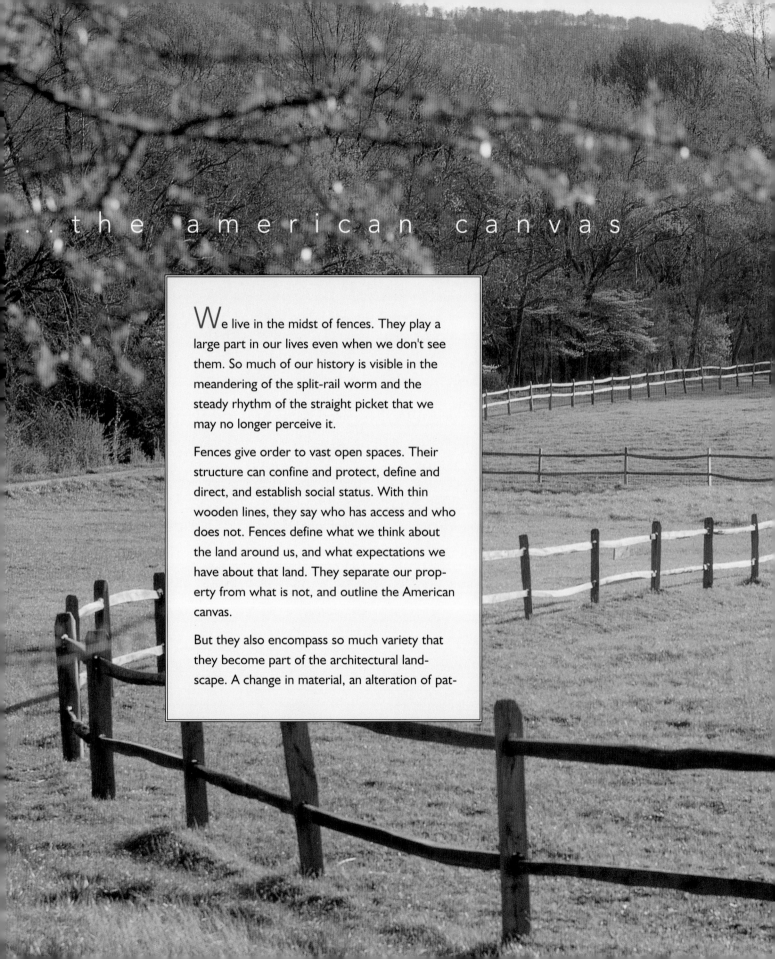

We live in the midst of fences. They play a large part in our lives even when we don't see them. So much of our history is visible in the meandering of the split-rail worm and the steady rhythm of the straight picket that we may no longer perceive it.

Fences give order to vast open spaces. Their structure can confine and protect, define and direct, and establish social status. With thin wooden lines, they say who has access and who does not. Fences define what we think about the land around us, and what expectations we have about that land. They separate our property from what is not, and outline the American canvas.

But they also encompass so much variety that they become part of the architectural land-scape. A change in material, an alteration of pat-

tern, a shift in angle can bring a backyard into the embrace of the home itself...or set it free to be part of the surrounding countryside.

How you use a fence has much to say about the order of things and how you view it. With the right planning, a fence can be a gentle reminder or a stern warning. It can be a guide, a limit, or a transitional edge. And it can create the functions and patterns that you deem desirable in the workings of the space around you.

Still, fences are structures, and as such they need sound planning and a solid foundation. When a fence is well thought out, properly designed, and carefully crafted, it leaves the impression that it belongs. And that makes worthwhile the effort expended in your energy, time, and resources.

The need for boundaries is part of our nature. Fences satisfy that need by joining the beauty of the natural environment with the best of human imagination and resourcefulness. Come, then, and enjoy the community of the fence.

When a fence is well thought out,

properly designed, and carefully crafted,

it leaves the impression that it belongs.

To the earliest colonists, the settlement of the New World was a transition far more startling than we can probably imagine. By the early 17th century, most of civilized Europe had long been claimed—domesticated for hundreds of years and thoroughly entangled in the influence of the ruling classes.

The opportunities for these emigrants must have seemed endless...but so too did the raw wilderness. The new land represented danger and the unknown as well as a chance to stake a claim and, by dint of hard labor, work it to fruition.

The fence became a prime element of survival. Tall, stout palisades enclosed the first settlements and guarded them from attack. Just as important, these fences protected the food supply from destruction by domestic animals. They prevented hogs from eating corn and kept dogs from attacking sheep. Lack of a fence could mean a shortage of crops, which would cause famine in the cold winter months. The issue was indeed critical enough to warrant specific and

detailed legislation regulating the construction and maintenance of fences not long after the first settlements were established.

Since planting fields and pastures were held in common beyond the "home lots"—small, individually fenced parcels that were at the time the closest thing to our contemporary concept of private ownership—fence-building and maintenance was also a communal effort. Individual farmers were responsible for keeping up with their assigned sections, and could be fined for not doing so in a timely fashion.

Eventually, officials known as "fence viewers" were appointed by communities to survey the condition of pasture fences. Even into the 18th century, when private lands became more commonplace, these viewers inspected fences for their sufficiency and legality. In the days before railways, public cattle drives put crops and private property at risk, and landowners could not sue for damages if they failed to maintain a "legal" fence. Specific rules on the height

of fences existed in many states, from a minimum of 4'6" in Maryland circa 1654, to an incredible 12' in Pennsylvania in the year 1700.

But even at this early period in American history, other elements were at work. The fence became a tool for taking land from the Native Americans already living on it and justifying control and "ownership" by the new settlers—a concept that was completely unknown to the native peoples.

As early as 1629, John Winthrop, first governor of the Massachusetts Bay Colony, conceived an opinion designed to validate the colonists' claim to the land. In essence, he stated that common land became private property through enclosure and improvement. The...."natives ruleth over many lands without title or property—they enclose no ground, have no settled habitation, nor any tame cattle to improve the land by." Their right, he stated, was a "natural right," not the civil right that the colonists had earned—and since there was more than enough land for both parties involved, the natives' way of life would not be encroached upon.

Yet encroached upon it was. Native Americans did not build fences to enclose livestock, as dogs were their only domesticated animals. Even though natives in New England and the Carolinas erected fences for fortification, and those in the northeast and Canada built effective fence traps to funnel deer and other game into stiles where their quarry could be slaughtered, none of these uses enclosed the land to the letter of the law.

Worse, the colonists allowed their livestock to run free, which destroyed the unfenced crops of natives. Disputes arose, and the indigenous peoples were eventually forced to themselves build fences, move on, or fight for their survival.

Opposite: Split, or "riven" pickets protected these 18th century homes and their gardens from wandering livestock.

Above: Double post-and-rail fence was sturdy, easily adjusted for height, and did not require deep post holes. The post tops were cleated or lashed together.

Right: Jackleg or buck fence permitted rapid fence construction with a minimum of preparation, as no post holes were needed. Only large animals could be contained with this type of fence.

Land ownership became a rite of passage into a society of freedom. When America was young, a landless man was not permitted to vote or hold public office in many states. The accomplishment of having fenced land granted one full participation in the public community.

The idea of "free range"—land upon which anyone could hunt and graze cattle—remained alive even as the notion of private property gained acceptance. It was Benjamin Franklin who contended that land ownership was what distinguished the American farmer from the European peasant. Yet carefully constructed laws simultaneously determined how much land was open to the public and who could use it. In fact, these laws controlled the opportunities available to the rich and the poor, the landed and the landless, and to those who were white and those who were not.

While 19th century New England saw laws requiring property owners to be responsible for fencing in their livestock, the rural South saw the closing of the southern range as a way to deprive Black Americans of their economic and suffrage rights. At the time, there were two hogs for every person in the South, and over 80% of the land remained uncultivated. Livestock was a commodity every bit as important as cotton.

Fencing and how it was used reflected basic beliefs about who had rights to the land and its resources. And philoso-

phies varied in every region of the United States. Court cases were heard and precedents set that were contradictory, if not sometimes ridiculous. In Pennsylvania, "the owners of animals must restrict them from going on another's land, and this applies to pigeons flying over or lighting on the land of another person..." A case in Louisiana, on the other hand, established that "running of livestock at large is lawful in open range areas and if a property owner desires to keep such roaming stock off his property...it is his duty to enclose the land with fence."

As the eastern U.S. became more populated and settlers moved westward, the question arose: Should farmers fence in their land, or should ranchers fence in their livestock? At the heart of the matter was money as much as livelihood. In 1860, farm fences represented a proportionally large investment of the U.S. citizenry. In an economy where the total value of all farms was placed at $6.6 billion dollars, the fences alone were worth $1.3 billion. It was estimated that to produce a crop, an investment of $1 in land meant another of $2 in fencing.

The zigzag, or "worm" fence, often referred to as the Virginia fence because of its omnipresence there, was by the latter half of the 19th century the most widely built fence in all of America, prompting the Commissioner of the U.S. Department of Agriculture to honor it as our "national

fence." Yet, though it was easy to build and required no nails (a scarce commodity in earlier times), it consumed extraordinary quantities of wood and took up a wide swath of space that could otherwise be used for crops. Even George Washington declared during his presidency that such fencing was "expensive and wasteful of timber."

Yet other events were occurring at the time which had an even greater impact on the country's development. Toward the end of the 1700's, the U.S. Congress declared that all public land must be surveyed before it was sold, establishing the Rectangular Land Survey. In this process, surveyors created paper townships of six square miles, divided into one-mile-square sections of 640 acres each. This grid began at the western border of Pennsylvania and eventually covered three-quarters of the continental United States.

The rectangles drawn on paper maps were brought to life by the building of fences and roads. The survey turned land into standardized components, ripe for enclosure. In the space of a few decades, over 1-1/4 billion acres of the

Opposite: A post-and-rail fence in Ola, Idaho constructed in 1890. The rail spacing was such to deter animals from going under the fence as much as from going over it.

Above: The worm fence required quite a bit of wood to construct. This example is nearly five feet tall, and fences such as these could stretch for thousands of feet to enclose pasture. Once called our "national fence", it consumed its way out of existence for practical purposes by the end of the 19th century. Inset: A joint detail.

Right: A colonial example of the use of post-and-rail fencing in Old Salem, North Carolina. This type of fence took some time to construct because of the mortised rail sockets and the need for well-set posts.

United States was up for sale, stimulating for the first time more profit in the buying and selling of land than in the actual working of it.

With farmers eager to move westward to settle on affordable land, the consumption of timber for homes and fencing reached a critical point. By the middle of the 19th century,

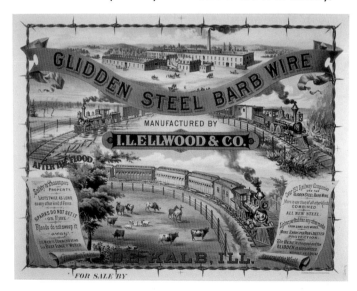

fences were becoming more valuable than the land they were meant to enclose. Clearly, wood had to give way to other materials, and between 1801 and 1881, over 1,200 patents were issued that in one way or another were meant to address this problem.

It was wire fencing, in particular barbed wire, that brought about the transition from wood to steel. Though timber was still needed for posts (the steel post wasn't developed until the turn of the century), the advent of barbed wire in 1874 allowed hundreds of thousands of acres to be fenced quickly and cheaply...and often illegally.

In the west, large ranchers fenced public lands and blocked public roads to the bane of settlement; farmers, in a westward wave, had already succeeded in closing the range in many areas and forcing ranchers to contain their stock. So the infamous range wars of the late 1800s developed, pitting cattle-drivers against farmers, ranchers against homesteaders, and sheepherders against cattle ranchers who both were competing for the same grazing lands.

Above: Braced posts and barbed wire fencing, tightened with twitch sticks. Barbed wire replaced wood in much of the west as timber supplies dwindled and demand for fence increased toward the end of the 19th century.

Below: A circa-1900 advertisement for barbed wire patented by Joseph Glidden in 1874. He and partner fence entrepreneur Isaac L. Ellwood put DeKalb, Illinois on the map as the home of the American barbed-wire industry.

Herd laws were ultimately enacted in some states that required the herding of cattle and the confinement of hogs, placing the burden of control on stock owners and extending the opportunity to settlers who could not afford fences to settle without risk and get down to the business of farming.

As small ranchers and farmers rejected barbed wire—both for its unnatural aspect and for its cruel method of control—other types of fencing were being developed. Even as wire was being strung, some ranchers experimented successfully with stump fences and living fences of trees and shrubs. By the close of the 19th century, barbless woven wire fencing

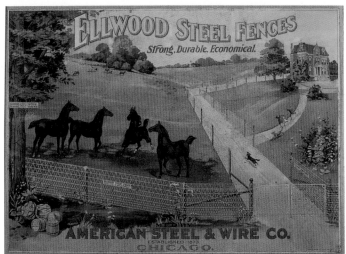

Above: Pine stump fence near Stoufville, Ontario in central Canada proves that even the most indigenous materials can successfully be used as fencing.

Above right: Crimped wire fence surrounds a farmhouse in Grundy County, Iowa, in 1940. By that time, steel posts were widely in use.

Center, right: An advertising poster for Ellwood Steel Fences used around the turn of the century. The house on the hill is the original 1879 Ellwood mansion in DeKalb, Illinois. American Steel & Wire Co. was one of the growing corporate conglomerates of its time; it held the lion's share of the wire market.

Below: Sturdy posts and welded-wire panel contain horses in this pasture. The wire fabric works best when the posts are spaced closely and sunk deeply.

(with both horizontal and vertical strands) had found a market among farmers, especially in the timber-scarce midwest, who came to realize that the supply of trees was running out. Improvements in quality and manufacturing techniques allowed wire fences to flourish and take the many forms we see today, including yard, lawn, trellis, and welded fencing.

But it was still farm fencing, with its task-specific organization, that first established the patterns of our rural and suburban landscape. Fences separated "home" life from "farm" life and, later, from "work" life.

For the American homeowner, the picket fence is the symbol of self-sufficiency, permanency, privacy, and a sense of pride. It has its roots, first, in the modification of the settlers' palisades to the livestock-excluding "picquets" built around private yards. It was also held, architecturally, to be the natural American adaptation of the wrought-iron examples seen on the estates of England and Europe.

This domestication of property—both public and private—proliferated through the nineteenth century. A stratified approach was adopted that placed several levels of fence around a site, the picket being the one at the center, around the house itself.

By the early 1900s, with wandering animals no longer a nuisance, a movement toward landscape design and natural settings prompted interest in open, grassy spaces between houses, with views unbroken by fences. By the mid-20th century, though, real estate developers were building neighborhoods in a effort to create—almost instantaneously—the sense of hometown community that had evolved on its own not many years before.

Today, fences are once again a central element in the revival of small-town life. Communities specifying fence design, right down to the color and sheen characteristics, exist in a number of states. The white picket fence has indeed become a fixture on the American landscape, if only to remind us of the positive aspects of property and pride.

Above, left: Through-mortises in the top rails and blind mortises in the lower rails house the pickets in this reconstructed fence and gate in Old Salem. The rails are, in turn, mortised into the posts.

Center, left: Curved-top bays and intricate turned posts typify the care and detail sought in fencing private property.

Left: The American Dream, personified by the fenced backyard and patio in Alexandria, Virginia, in 1943.

The white picket fence has indeed become a fixture on the American landscape,

if only to remind us of the positive aspects of property and pride.

SURVEYING + PLANNING YOUR SITE

Every fence has a function. And regardless of what it is—and several may be involved—it's important that you establish beforehand what you intend the structure to accomplish.

It matters little whether you're dressing up a tidy suburban yard or keeping animals from your garden—the planning considerations run a comfortably predictable gamut. To be honest, fences can be expensive, and the building task challenging. In order to make the job right and worthwhile, you'll need to do several things before you buy your first board.

This backyard area was carefully planned to accommodate several activities, including gardening within a dedicated space.

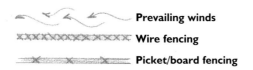

Prevailing winds

Wire fencing

Picket/board fencing

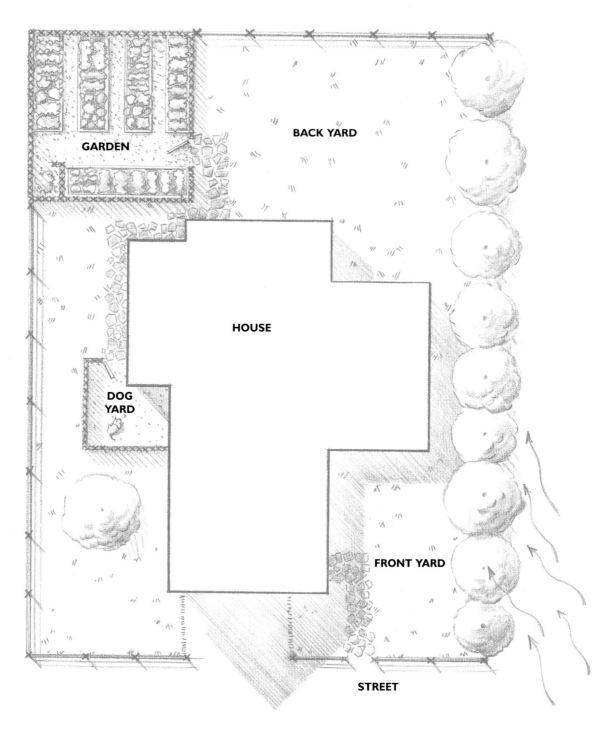

GARDEN

BACK YARD

HOUSE

DOG
YARD

FRONT YARD

STREET

1 . D E F I N E   T H E   F E N C E ' S   J O B .

Is it there to solve a problem, designate a boundary, or improve the appearance of your property? Other functions might include serving as a windbreak, a noise screen, or a physical barrier against intrusion.

2 . S U R V E Y   T H E   L A N D S C A P E .

Maybe not literally, but with detailed consideration. Be aware of things such as slopes, uneven terrain, trees, ditch-

es, and other obstacles that you'll have to contend with when running the actual fence line.

3 . C O N S I D E R   Y O U R   N E I G H B O R S .

And the building codes while you're at it. From a purely legal standpoint, it's important that you know the location of your property lines. If any part of your fence intrudes on your neighbors' holdings, it is you who will bear the responsibility of moving or removing it if there's an objection. Aside from that, it's just plain considerate to discuss with your neighbors beforehand what you intend to do.

In exchange for accepting a bit of input on design and appearance, you may enjoy the benefit of having a shared maintenance agreement—in writing—that will save you money over time. Lacking such an agreement, be certain that the new fence is entirely within the bounds of your own property, preferably with a buffer of a foot or so to avoid any questions or misunderstandings.

Also, some communities specify within their building codes basic design and construction requirements for fencing. There may also be ordinances limiting the height of boundary fences, and restrictions on certain building materials that could be hazards to the public, such as barbed wire or electric fencing in a residential area.

DRAWING A PLAN

The best way to start off right in planning a fence is to make a scale drawing of your property. It doesn't have to be fancy, but it does need to be to scale so that you can make an accurate representation of where the elements within your yard are, and how they'll fit with the proposed new construction.

A landscape architect does this every time he begins a job. You should, too, and it can be as simple as a sketch on a blank sheet or a piece of graph paper. If you use graph or grid paper, you can designate a scale and stick to it—perhaps one square will equal 2 or 3 feet.

Begin by either pacing out your yard or measuring its perimeter with a 50-foot steel tape. Once you've got the boundary lines down, measure and place the outlines of your house, any outbuildings, and other features within your yard, including driveways, paths, steps, garden spaces, and dog lots. Don't neglect to include trees, shrubs, and significant plantings such as hedges, because they will alter traffic flow just as a structure would. The image you'll make is a top view, which is easy to study and comprehend.

Do your draft in pencil, and double-check any measurements that you're unsure of. Then go ahead and darken or ink in the permanent items—your house, trees, and anything you simply do not want to or cannot move. You can also label the permanent elements outside your space that will have an impact on it: the street, the sun's path, the direction of prevailing winds. At this point it's a good idea to make a couple of photocopies of your sketch. You may decide to rearrange the smaller elements based on what you see in your plan, and it'll be convenient to have several fresh sheets to scrawl on.

With the plan on paper, you can now mark the existing traffic patterns. Keep in mind that traffic does not just mean movement between your parking area and the back door—it should also take into account children's activities, your dog-walking routes, gardening paths, and service access. As the children get older, their needs and patterns will change. Too, your interests may evolve and you'll be doing everyday things in different places. Most importantly, don't exclude other family members' opinions or make arbitrary decisions.

Above: This fence sets boundaries within the space.

Left: It's obvious how traffic will flow through these gated openings in the fence.

Below: This fence post has more than one purpose.

If the fence becomes a barrier to those within your family circle, its presence will only be resented.

Other elements are worth considering as well. Are there any views that you like to keep? Or, conversely, any that

should be blocked? Is there a source of noise from traffic or commerce that a fence could help to restrict? If you are a gardener, you certainly don't want to block the sun with a high panel fence too close to the beds, yet you may want to temper the effects of a prevailing wind with something less imposing.

And think about gates, now, before you begin construction. How wide do any openings in the fence need to be to accommodate the traffic you anticipate? Also, there may be slopes involved that will affect not only the swing of a gate, but the construction of the fence itself. If there are any steep or uneven areas on your plot, measure and note them in the plan.

Sometimes, the perfect plan can be thwarted by a rock outcrop, or a tree growing in the middle of the fence line. Unless you plan to move either the fence or the obstacle, you'll need to plan on making it an integral part of your new structure.

Above: The fence makes room for things of significance that came before.

Below: Elements from the house are carried through into the design of the fence and arbor.

MATTERS OF DESIGN

Later on, you'll see some examples of fence styles which will provide some detail and inspiration for your own fence building projects. But before you get even that far, you'll need to organize in your mind the individual elements that make up a fence's design...indeed, that dictate what it should look like in order to successfully fit within the environment you're working with.

The fit or balance that a fence offers in its surroundings is without a doubt the most fundamental part of the design exercise. If you ever study a fenced yard through squinted eyes, you soon realize that the structure complements its setting rather than commands it. A formal framed-panel fence would look startlingly out of place before a rustic, hewn-log home. But mismatches do not even have to be that obvious to take their toll—low fences don't often work with tall shrubbery, and a rough and rugged fence would appear sorry and forlorn against a crisp brick walkway.

You should, too, anticipate the effect that your fence will have on the density of its environment. Don't be surprised if the new addition makes your space seem more crowded—after all, you are containing your view by blocking it, perhaps on three or four sides. This is not as critical with an open or "transparent" fence, or if the fence line affects only a small

Finally, be certain to check how your plan jibes with the easements and setback distances required from property lines, streets and sidewalks, and other buildings. These specifics are available from your city or county building and zoning departments.

Above: Narrow, stylized pickets are the perfect complement to the narrow brick in the structure wall.

Below: The open lattice at the top of this fence relieves some of its solidity, which could be overbearing in a small space.

portion of the yard. But the fact remains that your fence will look better if it's given some breathing room, and that means providing some open space around it, either by siting it appropriately or planning beforehand to remove some shrubbery or plantings.

Keep in mind that a degree of contrast is to be welcomed, not avoided, when designing your fence. If you duplicated your home's structural patterns piece for piece throughout the whole undertaking, the effect would be monotonous rather than complementary. That's why professionals strive to capture just a detail, such as the house trim or its porch embellishments, and restate it as an element within the

fence. Too much contrast, on the other hand, is not encouraged, especially with regard to color. If anything is to stand out, let it be a building or hedge rather than your fence.

Proportion and scale go hand in hand when designing a fence. The former is the relationship of dimensions within the fence itself. Each section or bay should reflect a proportional balance that is almost a factor of two's: its width should be twice its height, unless you're enclosing a patio or garden formally, in which case the golden mean is a square. There are, of course, exceptions to this rule, but they are almost exclusively open designs such as stacked rail fences which provide more of a border than a barrier. The latter is

the dimensional relationship of the fence to the structure it's meant to enhance. A large, imposing house would appear overbearing to a light, knee-high fence.

Another factor to consider is how structured or formal you wish your fence to appear. This has to do not only with its construction, but also includes the ingredients of symmetry and repetition. The more uniformity and consistency that exist, the more the fence will suggest formality. This carries through to surfaced boards and perfectly aligned fasteners as well. Absolute balance in the positioning of a gate or the layout of a perimeter likewise says the same thing.

Consistency, however, is important in establishing the fence's rhythm in relationship to the landscape. Most of nature's features are curved, loose, and uneven. This is in direct contrast with man's structured fences, which tend to be straight, flat, and proportioned. You can resolve the conflict by allowing to fence to follow the landscape's lead.

Finally, don't underestimate the effect that a fence will have on perspective, and vice-versa. Especially in open spaces, a structure placed in the middle ground will have the effect of lengthening the background. And, a fence placed in the distance will naturally appear smaller than if it were positioned in the direct foreground.

Strangely enough, for a structure so large and robust, the fence does not require an overwhelming number of tools to build. Even better, the tools it does require aren't particularly expensive or complicated ones.

Don't be misled by the inventory that follows. Not all of it is necessary, because some tools are mentioned for their convenience or as an option to others listed. You can surely get by with less than what's on the roster.

The tools are presented by their function, which may be a little deceptive because—especially in fence building—they may be asked to perform several different tasks. Nonetheless, things are clearer when they're organized and flow from the beginning to the end.

LAYOUT TOOLS

Line level   Steel tape

Mason's line   Framing square

Crosscut saw   Plumb bob

Hatchet

Half the success of fence building is in accurate layout, yet the quality of these tools isn't nearly so important as how they're used. There's no point in buying junk, but on the other hand there's even less point in overspending for anything on the short list above.

The line level is a small vial encased in an aluminum or plastic tube that hooks onto a horizontal string line. Within the vial is a bubble that centers when the line is level. It's used to establish level heights and to true up rails and boards.

Mason's line is the small level's partner and an absolute necessity in laying out your fence lines. Nylon is the most popular, but old-fashioned white cotton remains superior, because it's supple but not stretchy. You might find a 200' ball of line at a good full-service lumberyard.

Even in today's power-hungry tool environment, the handsaw retains its long-earned place. One reason is its convenience, especially in fence building, where out-of-the-way locations and power cords don't make life easy. With a sharp saw, you can cut on the horizontal, vertical, or at an angle in a matter of seconds and be done with it. With this tool, you don't want to skimp. Look for a 26" crosscut saw (the kind with the teeth splayed out in alternating directions) with a wooden handle that's comfortable in your grip. The tooth count should be between 8 and 10 points per inch, usually designated as "TPI."

The steel tape will be the backbone of your project, small as it is, for if measurements aren't taken correctly, the fence will be skewed in the end. Even though the tape is a mea-

what digging tools?

The most physically taxing part of building a fence is excavating the postholes. And unless you're digging just a couple of holes in soft soil, a spade simply will not get the job done.

Its blade is not designed to remove earth in a confined space, and the result of trying to make it do so will only produce an aching back and a hole that's far too wide for its depth.

The ideal posthole is straight up and down, or—if needed for anchors—wider at the bottom than at the top. To dig a hole like that, a clamshell digger is needed. You've seen the tool—it has two long, parallel handles and a pair of hinged blades at the bottom shaped somewhat like the shells of a clam, only longer, with sharpened tips.

At nearly ten pounds, it has enough weight to sink itself into the soil when dropped from a height of 2' or so...at least in theory. In practice, most users end up banging the blades into hard soil, then wrenching them to freedom with a moderate load of dirt intact. Pushing the handles together opens the blades for digging, and pulling them apart traps the soil so it can be removed.

You may rent a posthole digger, in which case you'll probably get a decent, heavy-duty tool built to stand up to the abuse that a rental item frequently sees. If you opt to buy one—not such a bad idea if you've got dozens of holes to dig—don't settle for an economy model with 4' handles and flimsy, unsharpened blades. What you want is a 6' digger with blades 5-1/4" wide and 9" long. The hinge assembly and stops should be thick and sturdy, with solid rivet pins. The shovel ends will be sharpened, and the handles comfortably dense and about 60" long. You can expect to pay about $40 for a good working posthole digger.

If you really want to get serious, professional diggers are available from contractors' and nursery supply catalogs that have replaceable hardened steel blades and sturdy fiberglass handles, and come in a 7" width and an 8' overall length. Modified designs are also made to work in rocky soil.

Rarely, however, will you need to go to that length to dig a hole. If you keep a small file on hand to dress up the edges of your clamshell tips every once in a while, make a habit of cleaning the shovel's surfaces after each day's use, and conscientiously coat the metal with kerosene or a light motor oil to discourage rust, you'll be pleasantly surprised at how much easier digging can be.

suring tool, it's listed with the layout items because it is one of the first things you'll use. A name-brand 1"-wide by 16' self-retracting steel tape is adequate for the work you need to do. Because of its width, the tape is stiff enough to extend some distance from the housing without sagging. A perforated hook at the end of the tape allows you to catch a corner of a post or board to get a quick reading. The whole package measures only about 1-½" X 2-½" X 2-½".

For the initial work, a large framing square can be very helpful in establishing right angles at corners and taking quick measurements. Made of steel or aluminum, this carpenter's angle has one 24" leg and one 16" or 18" leg. An inch scale broken down into ⅟16ths is stamped along the edge of each leg.

A plumb bob is a curious little helper that instantly becomes useful when gauging the position of post holes from a taut line. It's a cylindrical weight with a string centered in one end and a sharp point at the other. When suspended from the string at any spot on the line, the bob will point to the place on the ground directly beneath the spot. The "plumb" part of the name comes from its ability to determine the vertical truth of a post or other upright member.

A small hatchet may not be a necessity, but it's a handy tool for trimming and sharpening the stakes you'll use in your layout work. The flat back of a traditional hatchet (or the formed hammer head of a construction hatchet) can be used to drive those stakes into the ground.

SETTING TOOLS

Posthole digger *Sledge*

Star drill *Tampiong bar*

Level

Once you've strung your lines and laid out your site, the most laborious part of fence building begins. Digging holes and setting posts isn't a joy under any circumstances, but with the correct tools, it doesn't need to be absolute drudgery. The five items on the list are all you'll need unless, of course, you plan to hire out the rough work.

A posthole digger is the crux of the entire setting operation. What you want is the clamshell type, the half-cylinder shovels hinged near the top and fastened to a pair of long ashwood handles. This simple tool can make great progress in most every type of soil, unless you encounter rocks; they'll be dealt with by the next tool. Don't bother with the auger type of digger unless you'll be working in sandy or soft soil. You can, however, invest in the rental of a power auger, a large earth drill with handles, driven by a gasoline engine.

Star drills are supposed to be used to enlarge and split a hole in rock previously drilled by a masonry bit. But powered rock-cutting bits require electricity, which is often in short supply at the far end of the intended fence line. The manually hammered star drill will still do passably well on its own, creating a socket for a metal pin fastened to the bottom of the post, or sometimes simply splitting off a chunk of

rock that's in the way. A 1/2" by 8" or 12" star drill has a hardened four-tooth tip that's hammered, then rotated, then hammered again...and again...and again, until the job is done.

A small sledge or steel mallet is what you'll need to drive that drill with any force. A 20-ounce claw hammer is too lightweight, and awkward in tight places. The right sledge will have at least a 2-1/2-pound head and a handle no greater than 15" or so in length.

The tamping bar can be as simple as a four-foot 2 X 4 ripped down the middle or as formal as a steel pry bar. The latter can double as a rock-mover if you need one, but the tamper's purpose is to compact the soil around a newly set post. A capped section of 1-1/2" Schedule 40 pipe, a cutoff car axle, or just about anything long with a blunt end and some weight to it will do.

Now we're talking about a true carpenter's level here, not just a small spirit level. Ideally, your level will be 24" long, and have an aluminum or steel frame, unless you've inherited one of those lovely old-timers graced with hardwood and brass. In a pinch, you can use what's known as a torpedo level, less than 12" long with a 45-degree vial built in.

MEASURING TOOLS

Combination square *Marking gauge*
Pencil compass *Sliding bevel*

These are the finer instruments you can use in the work-shop phase, or out in the field if you're marking and fitting components on site. Experienced woodworkers will recognize that many other tools could be used to render shapes and create visual effects, but this list is a fair and uncompli-cated sampling.

The combination square is one of the few multiple-use tools that really works the way they say it will. It has a 12" blade with inches marked off in 1⅛" and ¹/₁₆" increments on both faces. The cast stock has one square and one 45-degree shoulder, designed to slide along the blade and lock down with a thumbscrew. It's perfect for marking quick perpendic-ular or angled cutting lines and for gauging depth from a given edge.

A pencil compass comes in handy for marking circles and radiused arcs when designing a picket pattern, for example. It doesn't have to be a fancy one—even a child's school compass will work well for this purpose. One leg has a point that serves as a pivot and the other holds a pencil for mak-ing the arc.

The marking gauge may not be used by everyone, but it does allow you to scribe a clean line into the grain of wood using an established edge as a guide. A mortise point on the gauge permits you to lay out mortises exactly so they can be chiseled out in the right location. This is a bench tool that's used more in the workshop than on site.

A sliding bevel is another bench tool that's most often used in cabinet work, but can be helpful for duplicating lines and angles. The bevel blade is about 9" long and locks down against the tool's stock at any angle between 0 and 180 degrees. It's set to correspond to an existing angle, then positioned to carry that angle to a new location for marking and cutting.

BUILDING TOOLS

Circular saw   *Mortise chisel*   *Drill bits*

Jigsaw   *Mallet*   *Spade bits*

Router and bits   *Framing hammer*   *Spring clamps*

Hole saws   *Cordless drill*   *Square-nose cutting pliers*

Driver bits

These represent the workhorses of any fence building project. For the most part, they are everyday tools that people might even have on hand as part of a household collection for home repair. With the exception of the router and its bits (which would be needed only if you plan to embellish posts or other pieces with design elements) the tools on the list are common and relatively inexpensive.

The circular saw is a hand-held motor-driven saw with a 7-1/4" blade, though other diameter sizes are made for specialty work. Try to avoid anything smaller, such as a 4½" or 5" trim saw, because you'll need the full diameter to cut deeply into 4 X 4s and posts. Of course, the saw must have a shoe, or bottom plate, that adjusts between 45 and 90 degrees for bevel cuts, and should have a carbide-tipped combination blade for performance.

For cutting curves and free-form shapes in wood no thicker than 1-½", the jigsaw is your tool of choice. Also called a sabre saw, its reciprocating bayonet-style blade moves very rapidly and is thin enough to literally turn corners. Heat buildup can be a problem with these blades, because it warps the steel and can thus alter the cut. Working slowly, in dry wood, minimizes this complication.

A router's job is to cut grooves and slots, make rabbets, and shape edges in wood. For fence building, this work is mostly decorative. The cutting itself is done by a bit held in a collet on the end of the motor shaft. A smooth, flat base plate keeps the bit level and allows for depth adjustment. Handles on the motor housing permit the operator to control the direction of cut. The best router for fence work would have a ½" collet rather than the lighter-duty ⅜" socket, and requires a motor rating of at least 12 amperes.

The design and shape of the individual router bits designate what form the finished edge or groove will take. There exist over 200 router-bit styles, though a half-dozen will suit the needs of most nonprofessional builders.

Hole saws are simply saw blades drawn into a circle and equipped with arbors at the upper end. The arbor fits into the chuck of a power drill or drill press, and the saw bores the appropriate-sized hole. Diameters can range from ½" to over 4".

The mortise chisel is heavier and thicker-bladed than the standard cabinet chisel. It has to penetrate and lever waste from tough mortise cuts. The best style for this type of work has a high-impact handle and a ¾"-wide blade. Overall length should be between 10" and 12".

A mallet will be needed to drive the chisel for deep mortise work. A hardwood or a large plastic mallet will work, but many people prefer the feel of the traditional bench mallet, with a large head often made of beechwood.

Another hammer that'll see plenty of use is the framing hammer. A heavy steel, hardwood, or fiberglass body is needed for the rough work, and the weight should be at least 20 ounces. The rip-claw design does not have as exaggerated a curve on the claw and can be used for prying boards as well as pulling nails.

You'll find that even if your fence work is close to the source of an outlet, you'll probably prefer to work with a cordless drill rather than the more cumbersome plug-in model. Make no mistake, though—the 110-volt version packs more torque, but it also has the drawback of being more difficult to start smoothly when driving screws, unless you get one specifically for that purpose. Choose a cordless model with a ⅜" chuck and at least a 9.6-volt battery; newer 12-volt models are even better.

The driver bits to fit the drill are for sinking the Phillips-head decking screws that you'll use where you don't use nails. The standard size is a No. 2 Phillips, about 1-½" long. For more torque, look for a style with a longer shank. You may need to get a No. 3 Phillips driver for the larger (No. 12) screws if you use them.

Regular high-speed drill bits are pretty much a necessity when you own a drill. They're designed to cut through mild steel and wood, so they are fairly universal. For convenience, it'd be best to have a small 7- or 8-piece selection in a closed plastic case. Sizes range from 1/16" to 5/16", and larger.

Spade bits make the trasition from a ¼" bit to the larger sizes, and go up to 1-½" in diameter. They're designed with a center point and two flat cutting edges, and bore rough holes through wood in a hurry.

Spring clamps are convenient tools for holding work while you mark or drill. Other types of clamps are certainly usable, but a large spring-style—say about 3-½"—has plenty of strength and can be tighened and released without a lot of fuss and wasted time.

Square-nosed cutting pliers are handy for removing fence staples and twisting and clipping wire. They can also bend and cut nails and do all sorts of minor chores. Don't bother with small ones—the best size is 9" or 10" overall.

SAFETY TOOLS

Dust mask   *Safety glasses*

Leather gloves   *Ear protectors*

Even hand tools can be hazardous, since they can cut and chip just as effectively as if they had motors behind them. When working with wood, it's always prudent to be prepared for the worst and protect yourself to whatever degree you can. Eyes are most vulnerable, of course, but other body parts can suffer damage over time. And none of the items mentioned is so costly that it's not worth the investment.

Safety glasses are the one tool that you really shouldn't be without. For a total outlay of the price of lunch, you'll have the assurance that your vision will remain protected against all but the most forceful intrusion. The best glasses combine light weight and comfort with safety, so a wraparound design (that allow both the front and the side of the eyes to be covered) with high-impact polycarbonate lenses are the thing to look for.

Ear protectors are used to suppress the noise of power tools. It may not sound like a problem, but a loud router or saw can take its toll on hearing after repeated exposures.

Indoor environments exacerbate the problem, but using the tools outdoors does not solve it completely. Lightweight muffs with soft seals and a Noise Reduction Rating (NRR) of 25 decibels will keep you comfortably safeguarded.

A dust mask is necessary to keep fine particulate matter from entering your respiratory system when cutting and sanding wood. How fine? Material down to .5 microns, or five-thousandths of a millimeter, should be stopped by the minimum-level mask—or at least 98% of it should be. We cannot, in fact, even see individual dust particles smaller than 100 microns. A good mask will have a positive face seal and a yoke-type cradle for comfort.

Leather gloves are a cheap form of protection against splinters, abrasion burns, and accidental cuts. Heavy gauntlet-style gloves work well, but may not let you function comfortably. A better choice is smooth, lighter-weight pigskin or even deerskin gloves that permit a sense of feel through the material.

USING THE RIGHT MATERIALS

When we think of fences, we think of wood, and that, for the most part, is the material you'll be using in the preparation and construction of your fencing projects. Don't forget, though, that other materials—bamboo, wire, and by-products of wood included— are suitable candidates for fencing and may become an integral part of an otherwise wooden fence.

The range of materials is broad, and your options will be affected not just by what you like the look of, but by other factors that run the gamut from practical to possible. Take a look at the following elements and you'll see what you can become involved with in making a decision.

Locust has been a venerable fence-building wood for hundreds of years.

APPEARANCE.

Certainly one of the key elements in designing a fence, appearance isn't always easy to get a handle on. If you're attempting to restore the look of an older structure or garden and have an existing pattern or section to work from, the task is not that difficult, assuming you have access to the same type of materials and can replicate the cuts and details. If you are working to create a look, the job is a bit more challenging because your base of choices will be broadened.

MAINTENANCE + DURABILITY.

Naturally you should be concerned with how long your fence will last because you'll be building into it a substantial investment in time and materials. Some species of wood are more durable than others and certain materials will outlast others by a wide margin. These factors may be offset by cost, workability, and other elements addressed in this section.

COST.

Fences can be expensive, yet you'll still want to use the best material you can within your budget. There are a number of ways to cut costs if that's a prime concern. Buying in volume, negotiating on odd lots and remainders of usable material, dealing with salvage outlets, and using rough-sawn and recycled lumber are some possibilities. Expenses can easily get out of hand if exotic or specialty species are selected.

WORKABILITY.

If you are planning to complete the fence installation yourself from start to finish, you should be concerned with how difficult the materials may be to work with. Some woods—cedar is one example—split easily and must be cut and nailed with caution. Others such as black locust are extremely dense and difficult to nail into. You may be thinking of blending materials such as brick and wood, and so then must consider your qualifications as a mason.

AVAILABILITY.

Mass-marketing has made its impact on lumberyards and home centers everywhere. Viable commercial species—in

other words those that are self-supporting and profitable—are the ones that are stocked in America's discount lumber outlets. Southern pine, Douglas fir, spruce, and white cedar are well represented at these popular do-it-yourself stores. If you look hard enough, however, it's not difficult to find a more regional variety of species from a local source, such as a sawmill or an independent lumber dealer. These indigenous species have proved themselves over time to be reliable in the area where they're harvested and sold. You shouldn't overlook wood from these sources just because it isn't neatly packaged and graded. Some of the finest fencing around was erected long before the lumber trade was a multinational industry.

In one way, wood for fencing is not as critical as that for a building. After all, we're not living in it, it isn't supporting us, and there will be no casualties if it fails over time. Yet there is an aspect to fence wood that is very important to the fence—and that's how long it will remain in the ground before it submits to the inevitable effects of exposure.

Wood deterioration is caused by insects and fungi. Both these organisms need four things to survive—food, moisture, oxygen, and the right temperatures. We have little control over the last three elements, especially within a fence post buried in the earth. But the food source can be restricted, and that's exactly what occurs, naturally, in the heartwood of most species.

Heartwood is the dense, dead wood from the inner core of a tree. It contains aromatic oils and toxins that repel moisture and insects far more effectively than the sapwood which surrounds it. This core wood, though, takes a long time to develop, and most of the old-growth trees have already been harvested long ago. Today, most commercial lumber consists of second-growth timber lacking any substantial amount of heartwood.

Some species, as noted, still remain resistant to decay and insects, even as sapwood. These are appropriately marketed as fence wood because of such characteristics.

White cedar, either Northern or Atlantic, is a favorite for its durability and resistance to moisture and fungal decay. Though it's not insect proof, it can be treated for use in the ground. Cedar is common split-rail material and readily

available at lumberyards across the country. It weathers and finishes nicely.

Redwood is naturally decay- and termite-resistant and offers a beautiful weathered finish. Because redwood supplies are dwindling, it's a costly option that might best be reserved for smaller projects.

Locust has been an Appalachian fence-builder's staple for generations, but you must use caution to distinguish between black locust, the venerable woods-habitat fence-post species (sometimes called yellow locust by natives) and white locust, which sprouts to reclaim fallow open fields and does not have nearly the resistance of its like-surnamed kin.

Osage orange is a midwestern hardwood known, like black locust, for its ability to withstand the damaging effects of moisture. Its coveted for use as fence posts due to an in-ground lifespan of probably over 50 years.

Cypress, more accurately called baldcypress, is resistant to insects and especially to moisture decay, as it's indigenous to swampy areas in the Southern Atlantic and Gulf states. It's typically a local wood, unless you're fortunate enough to find a reasonably priced source outside the regions where it

grows. The heartwood ranges from a yellowish-red to a deep chocolate color, but weathers to a nice silvery gray.

Hemlock, the eastern variety, is often used for inexpensive utility fencing even though it's not particularly resistant to decay or insects. The wood is coarse and uneven in texture, giving it a hairy appearance over time.

Oak—but particularly the white oak group—is fairly resistant to moisture decay. It's a decent investment for above-ground fencing members, but should be treated in some way before using it as posts. The wood, of course, is hard and durable, and can be quite attractive if dressed in a clear finish.

Pine, the Southern yellow group that includes longleaf and loblolly, is a hard and durable species which has become the

Top: Pressure-treated lumber, primer, and several coats of quality paint are ingredients for a fence that will last for decades.

Above: Pine, stain, and a weather-resistant clear finish work together on this gate.

generations of fence builders

In a world where everything constantly seems to be changing, it is comforting to know that some things remain the same. Such is the way of the Emerys, who have been cutting posts and splitting rails in the shadow of South Carolina's Glassy Mountain for three generations.

It may have been Raymond Emery who founded the Emery Fence Company four decades ago, but his people had been known for working fences and harvesting the mountain llocust plentiful in the area for many years before that. As a boy of eight, Emery was trained by his father to drive the team of oxen that hauled the cut timber out of the draws and hollows of Glassy and Hogback mountains. Not too long after that, young Raymond was given a hardwood maul and a wooden wedge and taught to rive the arrow-straight ten-foot logs that would become finished rails.

"By the time I was 14, I'd been splitting rails for some years, and one evening daddy came in and brought with him a hard-steel go-devil, a maul, and a couple of steel wedges. After just a few swings, I remember telling him, 'well, we sure are coming up in the world'"! In his fence-making career, Emery has done everything from finding standing timber to hauling it, working it, and even peddling the finished pieces from the back of a flatbed truck. In all his years, he's never had to go home with an unsold load.

Raymond Emery continued to hand-split his wood with an 8-pound splitting maul until his age—and arthritis—made it difficult for him to heave his arms around in the great circle required to cleave the rails. Then he took up a 16-pound maul that with its extra weight let him just plunge the head to its target. Now, the elder Emery has passed the business over to his son Billy.

The family bids and consults on historical works and sends fence materials all over the United States. They have supplied thousands of feet of locust rails and posts for restoration villages to sites as renowned as Williamsburg and Yorktown, Virginia, and to places as far away as central England. Homesteads and settlements from New Jersey to Louisiana enjoy the benefit of the Emery's hand-split fence, and several authentic hand-built, peg-

jointed locust sheep hurdles are on display at one of George Washington's historical sites in eastern Virginia.

A number of years ago, Raymond Emery designed and patent-ed a 12-foot mechanical splitter that made the bread-and-but-ter part of his livelihood—building fence for everyday purpos-es—go easier. In the meantime, he also developed a method (which he wisely keeps close to the chest) for tapering rail ends and cutting mortises for post-and-rail fence.

Yet tradition is not easily forgotten, and many a time has one of the Emerys been sought to demonstrate the old way of split-ting rails for a historical event of some kind. Today, the elder Emery no longer cuts fence wood, but his perseverence and respect for the past has earned his people a place in the circle of fences.

The Emerys supplied wood for this reconstructed wattle fence in Yorktown, Virginia.

Joints, especially, are prone to water damage.

backbone of the Eastern timber industry. The heartwood of Southern yellow pine is fairly resistant to decay, but it is not as common commercially as it was some years ago.

Douglas Fir is the western equivalent of Southern yellow pine, and is sold nationwide as a lumber commodity. Like the Southern pine, its heartwood has a reputation for a

DIMENSION LUMBER SIZES

NOMINAL SIZE	ACTUAL SIZE
(inches)	(inches)
1 X 2	¾ X 1-½
1 X 3	¾ X 2-½
1 X 4	¾ X 3-½
1 X 6	¾ X 5-½
1 X 8	¾ X 7-¼
1 X 10	¾ X 9-¼
1 X 12	¾ X 11-¼
2 X 4	1-½ X 3-½
2 X 6	1-½ X 5-½
2 X 8	1-½ X 7-¼
2 X 10	1-½ X 9-¼
2 X 12	1-½ X 11-¼
4 X 4	3-½ X 3-½
4 X 6	3-½ X 5-½
6 X 6	5-½ X 5-½

moderate resistance to decay, but heartwood is not as plentiful as it once was. Both "Doug Fir" and "SYP" are candidates for chemical treatments that increase the woods' longevity

DIMENSION LUMBER

Stock from a lumberyard that is planed to a certain size is known as dimension lumber. The terms 1 X 6, 2 X 4, and 6 X 6 all describe wood that has been graded and dimensioned to a standard agreed upon by a select group of forest-products industry associations.

For structural applications, the use of graded lumber is important because building codes require it. For fencing, appearance is more significant and will account for defects such as knots, pitch pockets, and other flaws.

When you visit the lumberyard, you'll see that the sizes are stated in a three-number sequence. In a 2 X 4 X 10 sample, the first gives the thickness of the wood in inches, the second its width in inches, and the third its length in feet. But these numbers represent only the nominal sizes—accurate in name only.

More important is their actual dimension, or the actual sizes you'll be getting. Because wood shrinks somewhat after it's cut from the mill and dried, and because the planing or "surfacing" process removes even more wood, up to ½" of material is lost in thickness and width by the time it arrives at the retailer; lengths will remain true. The *Dimension Lumber Chart* indicates the nomimal and actual sizes you can expect when buying lumber. The moisture content of the wood you buy will affect its performance and stability. The more moisture within the wood, the more likely it is to warp, cup, and split as it gives up that moisture to the air, especially if it's exposed to direct sunlight.

When wood is first cut, it may have a moisture content well over 50%. As water is drawn from the hollow cell cavities through evaporation, the moisture level decreases without changing the wood's dimensions until it reaches approximately 28%. At that point, the water migrates from the swollen cell walls, which does affect shrinkage and warping.

Therefore, it's to your benefit to try to use air-dried, and preferably kiln-dried, wood if possible. The labeling stamps for moisture content are as follows: S-GRN is green, unseasoned wood with a moisture content of 20% or greater. S-DRY is the standard lumberyard fare, sold with a moisture content of 19% or less. There is also an MC-15 label, used mostly for hardwoods and flooring that requires a 15% or less level of moisture.

Some guidance to terminology may be helpful, especially if you're a novice to the lumber business. A piece 1" or 2" thick and between 2" and 6" wide is a strip. Stock less than 2" thick and from 8" to 12" in width is called a board. The dimension lumber for framing is 2" to 5" thick and up to 12" wide. Timbers are 4" or greater on their smallest side.

The junctures at the pickets and rails of this fence are prone to moisture collection. The wood must be pressure treated, or of a species that's resistant to moisture damage.

TREATED WOOD

It was mentioned earlier that certain species of wood—cypress, black locust, and redwood to name three—are naturally quite resistant to decay. But those species are either regional in nature, or sold at a premium due to their limited quantity. The commercial species that are prominent in the marketplace—Southern yellow pine and Douglas fir—are, unfortunately, not as resistant to damage, and must be chemically treated to increase their longevity and make them more usable in permanent outdoor situations.

There are two general categories of preservative used to treat wood: oils, such as creosote and pentachlorophenol solutions in petroleum, and chemical salts that are applied as waterborne solutions. The lumber that you buy commercially will most likely be treated using the second method, one, because it's more effective, and two, because the treatment doesn't affect the wood's appearance and paintability as an oil-based treatment does. Wood so processed is known as pressure-treated, or "PT" wood in lumberyard parlance.

With the waterborne method, preservatives are forced under pressure or by vacuum-pressure into the cells of the wood, where they shield against the onslaught of wood-destroying organisms. According to the U.S.D.A.'s Forest Products Laboratory, the life expectancy of wooden structures treated in this way can be increased five- or tenfold.

The success of the treatment depends not only on the effectiveness of the preservative, which varies considerably, but also on the method used to introduce the chemical, and in part on the species of the wood being treated as well. Some woods are naturally more resistant to absorption than others.

Pressure-treated wood is classified by how it is to be used—above-ground or in contact with the ground. There's also a differentiation made between structural wood, used in decks and buildings, and general utility wood. What determines this difference is the retention, in pounds per cubic foot, of chemicals within the woods' structure. Above-ground applications require a density of only .25 lbs. per cubic foot, where a structural member in ground contact needs .60 lbs./cu.ft. Posts buried in the ground are rated at .40 lbs./cu.ft. because they are not supporting a building structure.

These ratings should be printed on a tag stapled to the end grain of the lumber you're buying. If not, be sure to ask the dealer for further clarification before you make your purchase. Depending on the grading organization, the ratings may simply be labeled LP-2 for above-ground use, and LP-22 for below-ground use. To be safe, professional fence builders specify below-ground lumber even for fencing members placed within half a foot of the soil.

Waterborne preservatives include acid copper chromate (ACC), ammoniacal copper arsenate (ACA), and three types of chromated copper arsenate (CCA). Two other preservatives—chromated zinc chloride (CZC) and fluor chrome arsenate phenol (FCAP)—are also used, mainly for above-ground applications.

For the purposes of building a fence, the CCA-treated woods are the best choice for a number of reasons. Economy is one; on a cost-per-year basis, it makes sense to spend an additional 25% or so to get a post that will most likely last your lifetime. Workability is another, for the CCA salts usually don't leave a residue on the surface, and so wood treated in this way can be painted and cut without special preparation. And, although no treatment is absolutely leachfree, the chromated copper arsenates are probably one of the most stable treatments available. As long as you're not growing vegetables right alongside a treated post or trellis, there should be no major environmental concerns.

Having said that, please be aware that there are some guidelines to using treated wood of any kind. First, you shouldn't cut it without wearing a dust mask, for you don't want the particulate residue in your lungs. (Common sense would apply this to any wood, especially red cedar, which can be toxic when inhaled.) Secondly, you should never burn treated-wood scraps, as combustion heat releases normally stable chemical bonds. Rather, bury them in an approved landfill. Finally, you can avoid possible reaction or being sensitized to the chemicals by wearing leather gloves when you work with treated wood. Wash your hands before eating, and wash the clothing you work in separately from other laundry. More specific safety and handling information is available in a consumer tip sheet from the dealer where you buy pressure-treated wood products.

Is it possible to treat posts and framing members yourself? Nowhere near to the degree of perfection that the commercial processors enjoy. First of all, hand-brushed or even soaked timbers will not fully absorb any chemical without it being forced into the wood cells. A low moisture content in the wood helps, but the treatment is still superficial by comparison. Bacteria and moisture within the core of the wood will work from the inside out to destroy it in a relatively short amount of time.

Equally important, some of the most effective treatments are no longer available to the individual as off-the-shelf purchases. As an example, pentachlorophenol was a popular antidecay agent until the Environmental Protection Agency established that it is a potential groundwater contaminant. Within the past ten years, borate salts have been marketed

under a trade name to provide a benign, but less effective, substitute for chemicals such as these.

ROUGH-SAWN LUMBER

Rough or mill-sawn lumber is a very viable option for the fence builder who has access to it. Generally, rural communities or those in the extended suburbs are close enough to a source of timber that it won't be impossible to locate one of the small, independently owned sawmills that seem to flourish anywhere trees are to be cut.

These entrepreneurial operations usually don't answer to lumber associations, but are rather answering a local need with native products. Some may specialize in pallet manufacturing, siding, or even fence materials. Here, indigenous woods with a rough finish are the norm. Often, established outfits will have the capabilty to dress, or plane, your lumber, but don't always count on it. You can, however, usually find a supply of air-dried stock, as long as you're willing to work with the sizes that are available.

Rough-sawn lumber is cut more closely to—sometimes even larger than—nominal dimension. This may reflect a lack of precision in the equipment, or simply a lack of interest in managing the bottom line to the gnat's eye.

No matter—sawmill wood is sold by the board foot, which is the long-established measure of wood content. Each unit is equivalent to a board measuring 1" thick by 12" wide by 12" long. You pay for 144 cubic inches of wood, even if the stock is slightly less than 1" thick or just shy of 12" wide. Anything over the limit is figured to the next larger dimension. Thickness is measured in $1/4$" graduations, expressed as a fraction, so a 1-$1/4$" board is called $5/4$" stock.

By this rule, 10 board feet of lumber is a ten-foot 2 X 6 or 15' of 1 X 8. To calculate board feet, multiply the thickness by the width in inches, then multiply by length in feet and divide by twelve. The *Board Footage Chart* gives totals, rounded to the nearest third, for various sizes and lengths of lumber.

LUMBER SIZES AND BOARD FOOTAGE

NOMINAL SIZE	BOARD FOOT @ LENGTH IN FEET				
(inches)	8	10	12	14	16
1 X 2	1-⅓	1-⅔	2	2-⅓	2-⅔
1 X 3	2	2-½	3	3-½	4
1 X 4	2-⅔	3-⅓	4	4-⅔	5-⅓
1 X 6	4	5	6	7	8
1 X 8	5-⅓	6-⅔	8	9-⅓	10-⅔
1 X 10	6-⅔	8-⅓	10	11-⅔	13-⅓
1 X 12	8	10	12	14	14
2 X 4	5-⅓	6-⅔	8	9-⅔	10-⅔
2 X 6	8	10	12	14	16
2 X 8	10-⅔	13-⅓	16	18-⅔	21-⅓
2 X 10	13-⅓	16-⅔	20	23-⅓	26-⅔
2 X 12	16	20	24	28	32
4 X 4	10-⅔	13-⅓	16	18-⅔	21-⅓
4 X 6	16	20	24	28	32
6 X 6	24	30	36	42	48

SELECTING LUMBER

The quality of commercial wood has deteriorated noticeably in a generation. What used to be just passably fair timber is now good stock, and truly top-notch wood is sold at a premium. A lot of the blame can be put on second-growth harvesting, but the practice can't be avoided. The best the retailer can do is accept the fact that a percentage of his stock will be unsalable and pass some of the losses on to the customer.

This is why most yards will allow you to hand pick through the stacks of lumber in search of specimens with limited defects. It's a good idea to wear leather gloves when you go to the wood yard, and prepare to dig deeply into the piles if need be. Someone to help at the other end is a definite plus.

Dimension lumber often comes in bundles, and the metal straps gouge the edges of the wood at the corners. These boards, of course, should be avoided. Just as often, the boards at the top of the pile—and those few left at the bottom—are what was rejected by others as being deformed, decayed, or damaged in some way.

There are several kinds of defects you should be aware of when picking lumber. *Knots* are obvious but often not a structural problem unless they're large or loose. A dark ring of encasing bark around the knot suggests that it might come loose over time, weakening a post or fence board.

Decay is also apparent as a pecky gash in the wood, but not a serious problem unless it's deep or if appearance is crucial.

Crook and *bow* are warpage in two directions. The former describes an edge out of line, and the latter a flat face that's bent. It's usually caused by improper stacking and drying practices. *Cupping* is warpage in the third direction, across the board from edge to edge.

Checks are separations of the wood fiber resulting from a growth defect, selection from a slope, or too-rapid curing. More serious checks develop into splits. Boards with major

Look the board over for other defects, and examine the grain patterns at the end cuts. Tight, closely spaced grain is best; as the grain gets farther apart, the wood gets weaker and less resistant to decay. Wood cut from the center of the log shows a circular ring pattern and tends to warp in the sunlight. Set aside the pieces you're comfortable with, restack those you're not, and search deeper in the pile as you need to.

LATTICE

Lattice is an ideal infill for fencing in and around the garden. The crisscross wooden slats are light in weight, yet each section's multiple joints make the structure reasonably solid. Also, the openings between the slats provide access for light and ventilation, and can be used as a foundation for foliage.

Lattice comes in prefabricated 4' X 8' panels, constructed of treated wood or cedar stapled at the joints. There's a standard grade, made with slats just under $\frac{1}{4}$" thick and 1-$\frac{1}{2}$" wide, and—at twice the price—a heavy-duty grade with thicker slats to resist warping and provide a more substantial structure. There's also a privacy lattice made with the slats

splits should be avoided completely. Otherwise, checked and split ends should be trimmed from the boards before use.

Wane is the deficiency of wood at the edge or corner of a board, caused by the natural profile of the outside of the log. Since wood with wane does not have four square edges, it can create problems when fitting and nailing.

Inspect each board by holding up one end and sighting down its full length. After checking one surface, flip the board one-quarter turn and sight again. Sharp crooks and bows are difficult to work with and should be avoided; graceful curves can usually be nailed straight in place.

Above: Lattice panel.
Right: Random-height slats with points.

placed closer together so the panel is not as transparent; because more wood is used, privacy panels are more costly than standard ones. Whichever is chosen, galvanized staples are a must to prevent popping and staining through the finish.

The panels, of course, must be supported in a frame defined by the fence posts and the upper and lower stringers. They're usually held in place with nailers—1 X 1 strips fastened along both sides of each edge to hold the perimeter securely—and topped with a broad cap to protect the wood and to give the fence an expression of substance.

LATH, SLATS, + STAKES

Lath is a standard lumber by-product used for shimming, trimming, and lattice work. Slats are similar to lath but are at least twice as thick, and without the rough surface that distinguishes lath. Grapestakes are about the same size as slats, but—because they're split rather than sawn—have a unique texture that's consistent but informal.

All these materials are available for the most part at full service lumberyards. Lath, because of its nature, is best suited to low fences and should be supported in a frame or against closely spaced stringers. It can also be used in longer lengths to make site-built lattice by nailing rows together at the joints. Slats, being more substantial, can be viewed as square- end pickets and mounted to standard stringers at a height of 6' or so, and spaced at a half-width schedule for privacy. Likewise, stakes can be fastened to the framework pointed end up and abutting each other to make the infill solid. Of the three, only slats are suitable for painting because of their surface; the others can be stained, or allowed to weather.

SPLIT CEDAR RAILS

Split rails of cedar—and occasionally redwood, locust, spruce, or white pine—are the basis for an entire genre of fencing that defined the American landscape from the time of the very earliest settlements. The zigzag fence, the Kentucky rail, the jackleg, and the common post-and-rail all have their roots in the ready availability of wood at the time.

Today, that's not the case, but the materials are still accessible from a number of sources. True split rails come in 6' or

Above: Turned pine rails and posts.
Below: Split cedar rails and posts.

43

8' lengths and are wedge shaped, with a 4" or 5" dimension on each side. Square (actually rectangular) rails are also available and are sized with 5" and 6" faces. Individual mills may make rails 9' or 10' in length.

Manufactured posts and rails may be rounded, with cut tenons at the ends, or flat ended, or shaped in more or less a wedge. These often are made of treated yellow pine and come in specific uniform sizes. Lumberyards and home centers are more likely to stock these manufactured fence components.

PLYWOOD + HARDBOARD

Solid panel fences and privacy screens have used plywood for years as the infill material of choice where rigidity and durability were a concern. Cost increases have reduced the popularity of this very formal fence material, but you should be aware that it's still a viable option.

Exterior-grade plywood comes in standard 4' X 8' sheets, but can be special-ordered in 10' and 12' lengths if needed. The standard thicknesses apply: ⅜", ½", ⅝", and ¾". You must use an exterior-grade product because the glue used to hold the wood layers together needs to be able to withstand the moist outdoor environment.

Plywood fence can be assembled in two ways. The first is to fasten a single ¾" sheet within a framework of sturdy posts and rails, and to hold it in place with edge nailers or trim molding. In this case, the plywood must have two good sides—termed A-A to indicate that both the face and back sides are qualified for appearance. The panels then must be painted or stained and maintained on a regular basis to prevent weather damage to the exterior surfaces.

The second method is to construct each fence bay like a wall, with interior studs. This allows you to use much thinner material for the faces, although it will require twice as many panels to cover the same section of fence. Plywood less than ⅜" thick should be supported with vertical 2 X 4 studs spaced 16" apart. With plywood ½" or more in thickness, the spacing can be increased to 24" centers.

One benefit of using thinner plywood is that it doesn't need to have two good faces, and it comes in a variety of styles.

Siding panels, for example, can be textured smooth, rough-sawn, or grooved in a number of patterns. They are also available preprimed and even prestained for convenience. And plywood of any thickness can serve as a backdrop for wood strips or a surface design of your choice.

Hardboard panels are another option that has evolved with the availability of new materials. There was a time when only tempered hardboard sheets less than ½" thick would be used as infill and painted (hardboard cannot take a stain and it must be tempered, or smooth on both sides, to resist moisture). Hardboard comes in the same sizes as plywood, so a single panel could suit for both faces. More recently, hardboard siding has become popular, opening a whole new venue for precolored and pretextured weather-resistant fence panels. Hardboard is heavy, and must be supported with a substantial structure to prevent sagging.

BAMBOO

Everyone knows bamboo as a rapidly growing grass with woody, hollow stems able to withstand a good deal of punishment. That attribute, and the material's warm, natural color, makes it a good fence panel candidate with a fair degree of personality.

The bamboo stalks can either be individually woven and secured to a standing framework, or, in a less exotic treatment, purchased as wire-bound panels and secured within each fence bay with nailers or trim strips. A cap is suggested with this method both to protect the upper portion and to tie adjacent bays together. Bamboo is naturally weather resistant and can be left unfinished.

Bamboo infill

WOVEN WIRE

Woven wire fences are commonly known as stock fences because of their innate ability to contain animals. They're easy to see, yet can be seen through, a quality that makes them desirable for a variety of uses in the neighborhood as well as in the country.

The original woven fencing was made of metal wire knotted together. Today, welded wire panels are the norm; horizontal lengths of wire are held together by a succession of uniformly spaced vertical wires. Typically, there are two kinds of woven wire product—field fencing, which is made specifically for livestock, and welded wire general purpose fence, which isn't as heavy. An exception is poultry netting, a thin-wire, hexagonal-pattern screen with 1" openings.

Welded wire panel on steel posts.

The distance between the horizontal runs suits the purpose of the livestock it was meant for. Usually, the spacing becomes smaller toward the bottom of the fence, both to control smaller animals and to offer the greatest strength at the fence's lower portion, where stress tends to be placed. Some designs use uniform, rather than graduated, spacing which adds weight and cost but may look a little neater. In field fencing, the vertical wires, or stays, are either 6" or 12" apart; in regular welded- wire fence, the stays can range from 1" to 6" apart.

Woven wire field fencing comes in rolls containing 330 feet. It's possible to buy smaller half-length rolls, or to simply purchase by the foot from a hardware or farm supply, though

it's more expensive that way. Other types of welded wire fence, including poultry netting, come in 50', 100', and 150' rolls. Fence heights (or roll widths) range from 24" to 72". Field fencing specifically comes in 32", 39", 45", 47", and 55" heights.

The wires' gauge, or thickness, determines the fence's strength. Four weights are available, from light-duty (14-½-gauge) to extra-heavy (9-gauge). For nonfarm purposes, the medium (12-½-gauge) is probably more than sufficient, if only because special equipment is needed to haul and install anything heavier. All but the heaviest field fencing has top and bottom horizontals two gauge sizes thicker than the rest of the wire, which is called filler. With welded wire and poultry netting, 16- gauge and 20-gauge thicknesses are common.

To protect the metal from the elements, the fencing is either galvanived or coated with aluminum. A galvanized zinc coating is most common for wire fence material, as the cost of aluminized wire is prohibitive except for special applications. A galvanized fence section of medium-gauge wire can be expected to last at least five years in a humid climate and up to ten or eleven in dry locales. For better performance, some wire products are available with a coat thickness of a higher rating.

Lately, a trend towards plastic mesh fencing has put that material on the retail market. It can come as mesh, similar to the design of the wire styles, or as patterned sheets. The up side of plastic roll fencing is that it's lightweight and comes in several colors. The down side is its susceptibility to ultraviolet degradation over time, which is a definite drawback for an outdoor structure.

BARBED WIRE

There is enough history and technical information on barbed wire to fill a book...but, thankfully, not this one. Suffice it to say that barbed wire—twin strands of parallel, twisted wire interlaced with two- or four-point, evenly spaced barbs—is really suited only to sheep or cattle on an open range. As if to reinforce that fact, a single spool contains 1,320 feet, or ¼ mile of wire. Livestock confined in small areas and active animals such as horses and goats can easily be injured on the fence wire's sharp points.

Truly, barbed wire is hazardous not only to the hides of livestock but to the flesh of humans as well. It will tear up skin as easily as clothing, and can be a special risk around children and pets. For this reason, there are ordinances against its use in most residential areas.

Smooth wire, or alternatively, multi stranded cable, is another story. It can be strung and tensioned at several levels between fence posts, or stretched between trellises to create an espalier or wired hedgerow. Most fencing wire is

Wire cross-bracing used between posts in addition to the horizontals.

either heavy (12-$\frac{1}{2}$ gauge) or light (14-gauge). As a point of comparison, a 14-gauge wire strand, at .080" thick, is slightly fatter than a fresh nickel. Do not be confused by the tensile-strength ratings of steel wire you might encounter. There are essentially only two kinds—low-strength, or soft, for general-purpose work, and high- strength for making true tensioned fences. The wire's tensile rating refers to how much pulling force it can withstand before snapping. Since high-tensile wire requires tensioning tools and a testing scale, it's more a product for the farm than the home, and can be difficult to handle besides.

Two strands of wire and four points took a momento from a passing visitor.

Wire fabric on a steel fence post.

SMART WOOD®

certified wood and sustainable forestry

If all you think about when shopping for lumber is how it looks and how much it costs, you might have second thoughts. Today, there are ecological aspects to buying wood that can no longer be ignored, even by home consumers.

FACT: About half the world's wood is burned for fuel, producing carbon dioxide, the "greenhouse gas" that's blamed for global warming. What's left of western forests is suffering damage from acid rain, insect infestation, and overt clear-cutting. And all over the world—most noticeably in the tropical rain forests, where over 1-¼ acres are cleared every second—soil erosion, loss of wildlife habitat, and species extinction result from harvesting of marketable timber and wholesale felling and burning of all other growth to make room for transient farming and cattle grazing.

This doesn't just affect the supply and cost of exotic imports, but also has an impact on domestic woods as well. Short-term forest management is a dilemma that truly has global repercussions because we all, eventually, will suffer for it.

One improvement is the practice of sustainable forestry, in which the forest ecosystem as a whole remains intact when timber is harvested. Portable equipment is used rather than heavy machinery, which compacts the forest floor. Road building is kept to a minimum.

The idea is to take just enough wood—and not only the very best—to allow natural regeneration, and thus a sustainable, long-term yield. Consideration is given to wildlife habitat, watershed protection, and the social and economic impact on local communities. Some suppliers also support managed plantations where alternative species are grown to replace tropical hardwoods and domestic species endangered by large-scale logging.

Beginning in 1990, several organizations have pioneered certification programs in which forestry operations worldwide are scientifically evaluated and certified as well managed. Scientific Certification Systems (SCS) of Oakland, California and the Rainforest Alliance of New York (Smart Wood) are two groups in the United States that certify and label by symbol forest products that meet the established criteria.

Will all this have an impact on your fence-building project? In all likelihood, probably not—unless you order by the truckload. Certified wood products are widely distributed, but not piecemeal, unless you're in the market for specific things like cedar shingles, hardwood flooring, or custom shelving. The point is, though, that "green" certification is working in the marketplace, and where there's a demand, growth is sure to follow.

A horse team and a simple wheeled arch made to accommodate draft animals minimizes impact on the forest floor when extracting timber.

Coatings applied to the surface of wood do more than just protect it from the weather. With color and texture, they can also tie together a number of small elements to create a single large one that blends with the surrounding site.

Because the finish you select will have some effect on the material you use, it is an important part of the planning process. And from a purely practical standpoint, the wood should be protected in some way from the withering effects of sunlight, moisture, and wood-destroying fungi.

Here's a quick thumbnail review of what you can expect from the most common treatments: The finish least likely to alter wood's appearance is a clear wood finish, sometimes called a water inhibitor. This clear repellent is often used on decks and railings to keep the elements at bay. Stains, depending on the type you use, have a somewhat muted, but definitely visible, effect on the structure's appearance and provide protection as well. The most obvious statement is made by paint, which is very protective and presents a crisp, bright look that works well if surrounding color themes are taken into account and respected. Paint requires a primer coat to assure a good bond.

Another option is bleach, which provides no protection to the wood whatsoever (and in fact helps weather it prematurely), but does lighten its color without hiding natural texture. And there's always traditional whitewash, an economical treatment rooted firmly in the past that still has some value for restoration work or to create a period effect.

The overview on pages 52 and 53 provides specific details for each of the treatments indicated.

How you apply the preparatory and finish coats is a matter of preference. If you prefer to use a professional contractor, consider the job done. But if you want to tackle it yourself, be ready for a somewhat tedious task.

Begin the job with the wood clean and dry. If you're adding on to existing fence, you'll need to prepare the old painted surfaces with a scraper and some medium to coarse sandpaper—Grade No. 80 or below. This isn't necessary if the existing finish is in good shape. In that case, simply wash the surface down with $1/2$ cup trisodium phosphate dissolved in 2 gallons of warm water. A sponge, sponge mop, or even a stiff broom will get the job done.

To remove mildew stains, the solution will need to be strengthened to 1 cup trisodium phosphate in 3 quarts of water with up to a pint of household bleach added. Treat the entire area evenly to avoid spotting. If you're trying to maintain a natural finish, you should know that a hot TSP solution can darken some woods. After washing, rinse the cleaned surfaces with warm water and allow them to dry completely.

Do consider renting a pressure washer from a paint store or rental supply if you're facing a big job. Hand-scrubbing 1,000 square feet of fence surface can be a tiresome chore. The typical washer uses a small gasoline engine and your garden-hose water supply to blend the correct amount of cleaning agent with pressurized water, which sprays from a wand-mounted nozzle at up to 2,000 pounds per square inch. A good housewash recommended by the paint dealer should be an effective cleaner.

Don't leave the store without a brief course in how to use the equipment or you can easily gouge softwood surfaces; a glancing spray is adequate in most circumstances and safer than a direct shot. Because the forced water is driven deep into the wood, allow several days for drying before beginning to paint or stain.

For painting, apply the primer coat with a broad, synthetic-fiber bristle brush. Experienced painters and professionals still prefer natural-bristle brushes for oil-based coatings, but the synthetics are generally best for all-around application and are easier to care for.

Synthetic-fiber brushes are made with nylon, polyester, and a two-part blend. Nylon bristles, being the softest, work best with thin, water-based solutions. The stouter polyester is better for heavier paints that would overwhelm a soft nylon bristle. That leaves the nylon/polyester blend, which happens to be a good working compromise for most finishes. Better brushes may have a variety of tip structures to choose from, but tapered or tipped (flat) ends are appropriate for outdoor finishing.

Choose a 3" or 4" straight-edge brush with a comfortable handle and a substantial, well-mounted ferrule (the metal wrap that joins the bristles to the handle). If you're working with particularly thin pickets or have a lot of detail work to cover, you'll need a smaller-width rectangular brush sized to handle those jobs.

The subsequent coat(s) can be brushed on, or rolled on using a short-nap cover, then brushed out. Ideally, paint will require two finish coats over the primer, though some formulated with a lot of hiding may do well enough with only one. Choose the width of your roller to suit the job. On a panel fence with a smooth surface and abutting joints, a standard 9" roller would be fine; broad pickets spaced farther apart could use a narrower roller and cover.

Another option is to spray on the finish with an airless sprayer of the kind that's become a popular item in hardware stores and home centers. This is an economical alternative to renting a compressor and spray gun, which is bulky and requires some experience for good results. Any kind of spraying should be performed on a calm day, with plenty of drop cloths on hand for protection of shrubbery and nearby structures. Airborne paint mist can travel a substantial distance and will adhere to anything it touches.

Depending on the type of treatment you plan to use, it's sometimes easier to do the preparation work before you actually assemble the fence. This method also works well if for some reason you need to build the fence in stages, with breaks in between. Precut posts and pickets can be set up on sawhorses and primed or sealed with brush or roller, then set off to dry. Even if not all the parts are precut, you can do the preparation work, and then come back after the fence is in place to touch up the cut ends before continuing with your finish coats.

Before starting the job, have your cleanup materials ready and your work area prepared. With sprayers especially, goggles and a respirator mask are a good idea, even considering that the work is being done outdoors. The standard woodworker's dust mask is not adequate in removing all paint vapors, so a cartridge-type respirator (effective at blocking particulates down to .3 microns in size) is what's needed, for an investment of under $30.

PRIMER

A primer is a preparatory coating that penetrates the wood and gives the following paint coat a surface to bond to. It allows the paint to be applied more easily than over raw wood, and likewise makes it easier to remove old paint coatings when the time comes. There are two categories of primers: Alkyd, or oil-based primers, which need to be

thinned with solvents, and latex, or water-based primers, which are ready to work with straight from the can. The alkyds are costly, troublesome to clean up, and can be a health concern in that the solvent vapors are both flammable and toxic. Water-based products are less expensive, clean up with soap and warm water, and are far less of a health issue. As for effectiveness, the alkyds have the edge, especially when applied to cedar, redwood, and knotty pines. Their oils help block wood extractives that tend to bleed through paint.

PAINT

Applied in one or two coats, paints protect wood from the elements and give a finished look to man-made structures. Like primers, paints come in two categories, alkyd and latex. Besides having the benefit of color, paints will conceal imperfections in wood (because they form a film on the surface) and can be reapplied without much trouble if seen to on a regular basis. Paints are available in various gloss levels, from full to semi-gloss to flat. The higher the gloss, the greater the durability, though harder finishes may be prone to cracking. As with the primers, oil-based paints cost more and are more troublesome to apply, but last longer than latex paints. Naturally, exterior paints are required for outdoor fences. With exterior work, the paint's potentially hazardous volatile organic compounds (VOCs) may not be as much of a problem as they are indoors, but are present nonetheless. Low-VOC products are becoming increasingly more available in manufacturers' latex lines.

CLEAR WOOD FINISH

This water sealer is a clear, nonpigmented finish used directly on the wood to protect against water penetration. On new wood, it can be applied without any preparation. Existing boards in good structural condition will probably have to be cleaned or bleached before application to give a fresh face to the wood before sealing it. When buying, make sure you distinguish between finish sealer and clear sanding sealer, which is used under paints and stains as a pre-primer preparation. If you do use a sealer beneath a stain, determine first from the dealer or manufacturer that the finishes you plan to use are compatible with the sealer itself.

STAIN

A stain does not offer the bold, finished look that paint does, but allows you to protect the wood and color-coordinate it to any structures or landscaping in the vicinity. Stains do not require an undercoat, so they can be applied quickly. For this reason, stains are better for rough-surfaced materials, and paints better for smooth-surfaced wood. Like paints, stains are both water- and oil-based. Stains are formulated in a wide range of colors and can be lightly or strongly pigmented. Any lighter-bodied stains will be more transparent and so will show the qualities—or imperfections—of the wood more clearly. They will also wear more readily. The heavily pigmented stains are closer to paint in that they're solid in appearance. But since all stains adhere to the wood by penetrating it rather than forming a film, any defects will still show up through the finish.

BLEACH

Strictly speaking, bleach (either sodium or calcium hypochlorite) is not so much a finish as a treatment used to take the "new" look off freshly installed boards. When applied, it has the effect of weathering the wood premature-

ly to let it blend with its environment. The process of bleaching is affected by sealers, so do not plan on applying a bleach product directly over a fresh coat of sealer. It will take several months for the sealer to wear down to the point where bleaching becomes effective. You should be aware that bleaches can be detrimental to plants and soil, so take that into account beforehand. Vegetation accidentally doused with bleach should be rinsed with cool water.

WHITEWASH

From a long-term maintenance standpoint, there are far better finishes than whitewash, but this inexpensive coating method is too traditional to simply ignore. The recipe for about ten gallons of a pleasant, satin-finish wash is as follows: Soak 1 bag (50 lbs.) of hydrated lime in 6 gallons of water to make a paste. Then dissolve 6 lbs. of agricultural salt in 3 gallons of boiling water. When the solution is cool to the touch, add it to the paste mixture. Finally, stir in 3 lbs. of white portland cement to bring the consistency to a thin paint wash. Apply with a soft-bristled brush. Since whitewash is caustic, it can be corrosive to metals (and wire fencing) and irritating to the skin, so wear gloves and safety goggles when mixing and applying.

Fences are held together, almost exclusively, by metal—nails, screws, bolts, and wire. Though it's true that a number of fences do exist that use no fasteners whatsoever (see woven and worm fences elsewhere in this book), most functional fencing benefits from the strength and convenience of construction that nails and screws provide.

Hinges and latches, too, are elements of convenience, both in the sense that they allow the gate to function, and for the fact that they require essentially no maintenance. You can imagine how long a gate would hang if it were latched with rope and suspended from leather thongs.

For the most part, though, people tend to choose their hardware for the way it looks rather than how it works, and that's perfectly reasonable, as long as some essential facts are established beforehand. The information offered in the next few pages will allow you to make the right decisions for the kind of fence you plan to construct.

FASTENERS

Nails, screws, and bolts are called fasteners—they're used to connect wooden components together and to transfer the load between them. Most people don't realize how many it takes to assemble a fence until they've had the experience, but suffice it to say that you'll be buying yours by the pound or box if you have any interest in economy. Purchasing hardware in small lots is never cost-effective, and only justifiable if you're making repairs or doing specialized construction.

Nails are by far the cheapest fasteners going and the quickest to install. All that's required is a hammer, and everything usually goes smoothly until it's time to remove them, which is a bothersome and time-consuming process.

The material used to make the nail should be your first con-

8 d FINISH

NAIL SIZES

SIZE	LENGTH	# PER POUND
2d	1 inch	870
4d	1-½ inches	316
6d	2 inches	180
8d	2-½ inches	105
10d	3 inches	70
12d	3-¼ inches	65
16d	3-½ inches	50

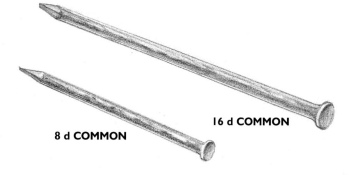

16 d COMMON

8 d COMMON

sideration. Plain steel or "bright" nails made of low-carbon steel are the least costly, but tend to oxidize over time, leaching rust stains onto an otherwise nicely painted surface. Stronger variations made with higher concentrations of carbon are called hardened nails and provide the strength needed to penetrate very dense woods, such as oak.

Either type will still rust, though, especially in the presence of treated woods, which contain corrosive chemicals, and certain wood species like redwood and red cedar, which are naturally corrosive to metal when moist. To alleviate this, you can use stainless steel nails, made from an iron-based alloy containing chromium, and blended with molybdenum and nickel. As the name implies, stainless nails are all but rust-resistant, but they're also very costly.

A good middle-ground choice, then, is galvanized steel nails, which, though lacking quite the longevity of their stainless brethren, are cost-effective and very resistant to corrosion over time. It's worth any extra trouble to insist on what's known as "hot-dipped" or mechanically galvanized nails rather than the slightly cheaper products that use an electrical plating technique. Galvanization—the process of applying zinc to the surface of metal—is more effective when the nails are dipped simply because more zinc gets deposited that way.

If you happen to come across coated or cement-coated nails, you should know that neither are they for use in concrete foundations, nor do they have particular resistance to corrosion. The coating refers to a resin applied to a regular steel nail shank which increases the nail's withdrawl resistance once it's driven. Their only benefit to the fence builder is that they would better resist stresses caused by using green lumber than a standard steel nail would.

Other nails you may encounter while shopping may be made of aluminum, brass, or even copper. These nails are used mainly to prevent a phenomenon known as galvanic action, which causes corrosion where two dissimilar metals join, such as when an aluminum strap is fastened with a steel nail. Yet, because all three materials do not rust, any could be used successfully as long as strength isn't a prime concern—though aluminum would be about the only practical choice due to the high cost of the other goods.

Building nails are made in a head-spinning variety of styles, but fortunately you should have to deal only with two or three. The nails most often used in fencing are common nails and finish nails, though box nails should also be mentioned because they see widespread use.

The business of nails is confusing first because of the nomenclature associated with them, and second because their sizes and lengths make no sense to the unknowing observer. The pennyweight system used to size and count nails came long ago from England, where it's believed that prices were based on 100-count lots. To this day, the penny designation still holds, right down to the "d" symbol used to denote it. Yet with so many specialized nails now in production, lengths and diameters may be different, even in the same penny sizes. A 16d common, for example, is $\frac{1}{4}$" longer and about 10% thicker in diameter than a 16d sinker. Still, the designation for common nails remains the standard; the accompanying *Nail Sizes Chart* shows the appropriate nail sizes. As a rule of thumb, use nails twice as long, or maybe a fraction again, as the wood you are nailing through. For fencing especially, it's better to use a thinner, shorter nail than to gain length through thickness, which will only split the wood.

The **common** is a plain-shank steel nail with a flat head and a four-sided point. It can be dipped to become a galvanized

nail, with no other changes. Don't confuse a common nail with a sinker, which is really a large wire nail with a tapered or countersunk head. Because the diameter of a sinker is slightly less than that of a common nail, its strength is slightly less as well. Sinkers are just a fraction shorter than common nails.

Finish nails are steel-wire nails with a plain shank and a small, tapered head. These nails are thinner than commons of the same size, but are of the same length.

Box nails are made of a lighter-gauge steel wire than common nails of the same pennyweight, but—like finish nails— use the standard penny lengths. Box heads are the same size as those used on commons.

Staples for fencing should be mentioned because they're used with barbed wire and welded and woven wire. By far the most common staples are U-shaped, though in some locales, short-leg, or "L" staples are available. U-staples have smooth or barbed shanks and come in sizes from $\frac{3}{4}$" to 2-$\frac{1}{2}$" in length, with gauge numbers decreasing appropriately as length increases. (The lower the gauge number, the thicker the wire.) The most common staples are 9-gauge, 1" or 1-$\frac{1}{4}$" hot-dipped galvanized.

1-$\frac{1}{4}$" **STAPLE**

FENCE STAPLE SIZES

LENGTH		APPROXIMATE #
(inches)	gauge	per lb
¾	14	480
1	9	105
1-⅛	9	95
1-¼	9	85
1-½	9	70
1-¾	9	65
2	9	55
2-½	6	25

Screws are used mostly for gate hinges and hardware because they provide a positive, long-lasting connection. However, it is no longer rare to see a fence built solely with screws, owing to the popularity of power drivers and the ready availability of quantity-lot screws in discount home centers.

Anymore, the best screws for exterior use are decking screws, which are self-sinking and specially coated to resist the rigors of life on a horizontal surface exposed to the weather. They follow the same schedule as traditional wood screws in number diameters and length (see *Screw Fasteners Chart*), but have Phillips-head slots for no-slip driving. Decking screws have flat heads with a bugle or tapered profile.

Regular straight-slotted flathead screws will work, of course, but are more time-consuming to install because they require drilling a pilot hole and don't take well to power drivers.

Screws with special eye-shaped heads, called **screw eyes**, are used to secure wire for bracing. They're available in generally the same sizes as wood screws, with not quite as much variety. Two or three different eye sizes are made for the same diameter.

For installing large hardware, lag screws are often the preferred choice. **Lag screws** are best described as bolts with a modified wood-screw thread. They come in hex- and sometimes square-head designs, either black, or with the more preferable galvanized coating. Sizes range from ¼" to ½" in diameter, and lengths from 1" to 8", in ½" increments.

Bolts are used mainly when it's appropriate—either for strength or appearance—to have the fastener pass completely through a wooden member and be secured from the opposite side. Some fancy gate hardware may require, by its design, that you use bolts to make the connection. Bolts are relatively expensive in the order of fasteners, and you wouldn't rely on them in a big way when building a fence unless it were a simple section, or for gate construction.

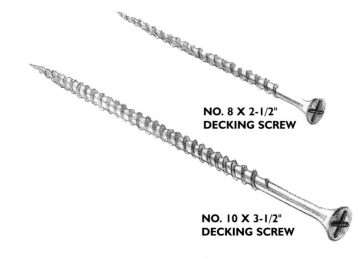

NO. 8 X 2-1/2" DECKING SCREW

NO. 10 X 3-1/2" DECKING SCREW

SCREW FASTENERS

Gauge No.	4	6	8	10	12
Shank diameter	7/64"	9/64"	5/32"	3/16"	7/32"
Lengths (by ¼s)	3/8"-1"	1/2"-2"	1/2"-3"	3/4"-3-1/2"	3/4"-3-1/2"
Shank hole drill	1/8"	9/64"	11/64"	3/16"	7/32"
Pilot hole drill	1/16"	5/64"	3/32"	7/64"	1/8"

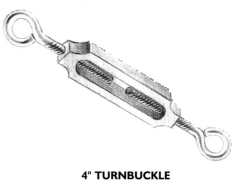

4" TURNBUCKLE

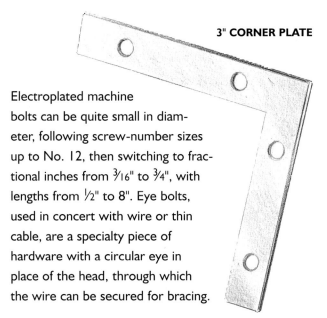

3" CORNER PLATE

Electroplated machine bolts can be quite small in diameter, following screw-number sizes up to No. 12, then switching to fractional inches from ³⁄₁₆" to ¾", with lengths from ½" to 8". Eye bolts, used in concert with wire or thin cable, are a specialty piece of hardware with a circular eye in place of the head, through which the wire can be secured for bracing.

Angled brackets, called **corner plates**, are often used to reinforce gate joints and other junctures that need some external assistance. They come in a variety of sizes, but those with legs of 3" or 4" in length and ⅝" or ¾" in width are the most common for fence construction. Make sure you use a good quality bracket if you use one at all, because the thin plating on cheap brackets will deteriorate in a matter of months, allowing the steel to oxidize and stain your finish.

Turnbuckles, along with eye bolts and wire, make up the bracing used in place of a solid wood brace. The buckle's frame and bolt design allows the wires attached at each end to be tightened by rotating the frame itself. They're manufactured in steel and aluminum for general use, and come in sizes from about 3-½" to over 10" in length, with bolt diameters from No. 8 to ⅜". The bolts have rings or hooks in the ends, and travel a total of 1" to 3" depending on size.

Calculating the quantity of whatever type of fasteners you need is not an exact science. The best method is to figure out the size and type of each of the nails or screws you'll be using for each section or fence bay, all components included, then multiply those by the number of bays you'll be building. Adding a fudge factor of 10% to 12% would not be inappropriate. Then refer to the chart to convert the number of nails to pounds, and divide by the box count to figure the number of screw boxes you'll need. Bolts and brackets should be hand-counted exactly.

HINGES

If there's one rule of thumb concerning hinges, it is this: Don't skimp on quality to save a few pennies. The underlying cause of gate sagging (and later failure) is inadequate hinges, and it's always more prudent to err on the side of excess than to use a piece of hardware that isn't up to the job.

If there is a hinge that you particularly like, but that may not be as substantial as you'd wish, you can always use an extra one on the gate's hinge stile. Normally, you'd use two strong hinges on gates up to 4' tall, and three on gates any taller. If the gate is any wider than 3', it's wise to use triple hinging.

Depending upon the style, hinge hardware may be black or zinc-coated. If you're building a top-flight or period fence, you may even choose a forged hinge custom-made by a modern blacksmith. When buying galvanized hinges, avoid the cheap, flash-plated zinc products that come with equally flimsy screw hardware. You really want a heavily galvanized hinge that will stand up to the weather, even if you have to go to a farm supply outlet to get it.

Hinge designs fall into four different categories—butt, strap, T, and lag-and-eye. Each has its own application and installation preferences.

The **butt hinge** is similar to a regular door hinge and may have a fixed or removable pin, the latter being more common on the better-quality hardware. It's designed to swing

Forged lag-and-eye hinge

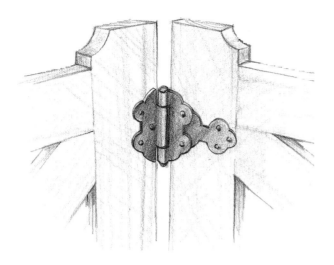

DECORATIVE STRAP

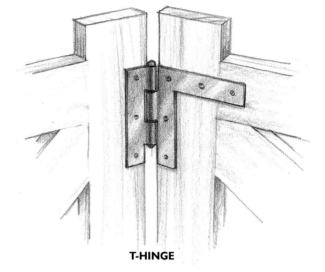

T-HINGE

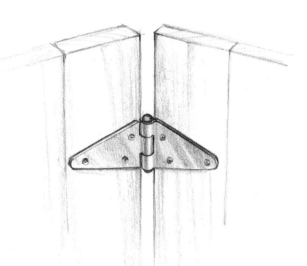

STRAP HINGE

LAG- AND- EYE HINGE

only one way. One leaf is fastened to the gate stile and the other to the gatepost. With this style of hinge, its possible to install it flat on the face of the gate, or to mortise it into the shoulders of the stile and post, just as it's mounted in a household door. Just the opposite is true as well—it can be mortised into the face or surface-mounted on the frame shoulders. Butt hinges come in a wide array of sizes, though something between 2-½" and 4" is appropriate for a gate.

A **strap hinge** is familiar to anyone who's spent time around barns and outbuildings. The tapered hinge leaves are longer than they are tall, and are permanently pinned together.

Their longitudinal design allows them to distribute weight amply over a greater surface area of the frame, particularly to the horizontal members. There is little point, aside from decorative, to use a strap hinge if the leaves are not going to be connected to a frame component. Strap hinges are surface mounted.

T-hinges are simply modified strap hinges, combining one long strap leaf with a rectangular butt-type leaf. The strap part fastens to the face of the gate, and the rectangular leaf can either be mounted (or mortised) to the inside shoulder of the gatepost, or surface-mounted to the face of the post, in full view.

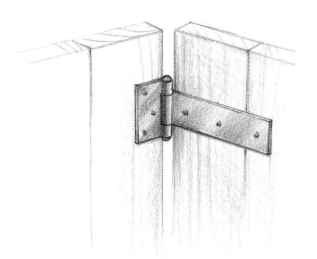

EXTENDED T-HINGE

Decorative T-hinge

LAG-AND-EYE STRAP HINGE

Lag-and-eye hinge

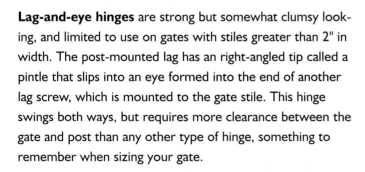

Lag-and-eye hinges are strong but somewhat clumsy looking, and limited to use on gates with stiles greater than 2" in width. The post-mounted lag has an right-angled tip called a pintle that slips into an eye formed into the end of another lag screw, which is mounted to the gate stile. This hinge swings both ways, but requires more clearance between the gate and post than any other type of hinge, something to remember when sizing your gate.

Hinges should be matched to the latch hardware when possible, especially when a particular pattern is chosen. Decorative surface-mounted hinges usually have a mated latch offered by the manufacturer.

If you purchase your hinges loose—that is, not prepackaged in a display card—you'll have to select your own screw hardware. Even if a package comes with screws, you'll probably want to save them for another project and buy heavier and longer screws for your hinges. The perfect screw will pass through the leaf hole without binding and penetrate the wood fully without penetrating the opposite face.

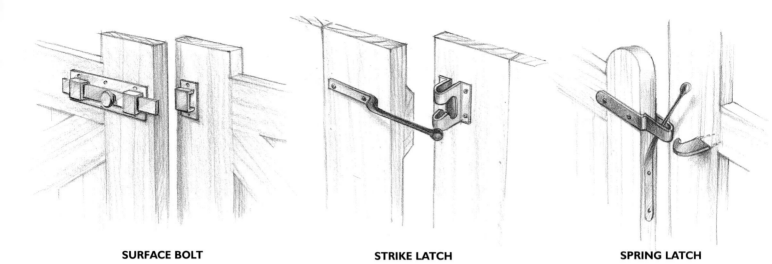

SURFACE BOLT   **STRIKE LATCH**   **SPRING LATCH**

LATCHES

Latches and catches follow the same rules as hinges: they should be substantial enough to tend to the job at hand. Latches, though, aren't subject to the same stresses as hinges, so they don't have to be overbuilt.

Like hinges, latch hardware can be black or zinc-coated, and forged hardware can be made to match as well. When buying galvanized hardware, the same cautions apply against cheap, flash-plated zinc coatings.

Latches come in three designs—surface-mounted, through-mounted, and loop. Because latches can be such an effective design element, you may have to suppress the urge to pick the best-looking one without evaluating its effectiveness. Sometimes, you can mount a latch in a creative fashion that will allow it to function well and still look just the way you want it to.

Below: Iron drop latch
Right: Wooden drop latch

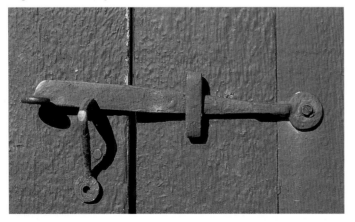

62

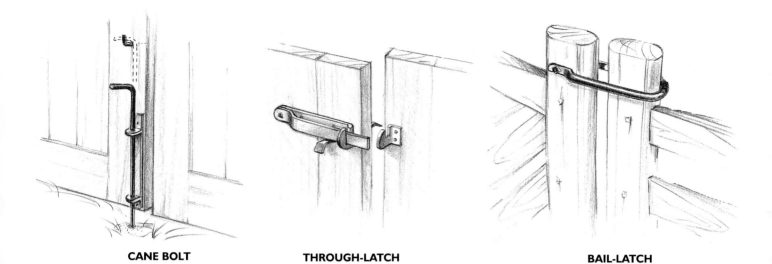

CANE BOLT **THROUGH-LATCH** **BAIL-LATCH**

Surface-mounted latches run the gamut from the basic hook- and-eye setup all the way to slide bolts and strike latches. Included also are hasps, spring latches, and cane bolts, which secure themselves to a fixture in the ground rather than to a fitting on the gate post.

Through-latches are simply surface-mounted hardware components that use a hole drilled through the gate to accommodate a piece of hardware—usually a rod, lever, or cord— that actuates a catch on the opposite side. Thumb-operated through-latches are common on paneled gates.

Loop latches, also called **bails**, are quaint and simple. They're just U-shaped straps that pivot on the gate post and drop over the latch stile of the gate, which is built with either an open frame or a rising stile to provide a snag for the loop.

Above: Wooden gate bar
Below: Gate bar on pivot

Make no mistake—a fence-building project is a big job. There are so many ingredients to a successful effort that it may seem, at times, like the whole thing should better be turned over to a professional. But, like any big project, it can be made much less intimidating by breaking it down into manageable components.

Just as *Building Fences + Gates* strives to define and clarify the many overall aspects of creating a fence, this one chapter aims to illustrate the particulars of construction itself.

The most important thing to understand is that all fences—in spite of how different they might look because of size, style, or construction—are really very similar. Regardless of outward appearance, there are only three major parts to any fence: the footing, the framework, and the infill.

Combined, these three components make up a bay, or section...and when connected to other identical bays, compose a whole fence. If you never taken the opportunity to study how a fence is put together, walk around and look at a few. You'll not only spot the repeating pattern just referred to, but you'll be able to see just how the elements work together to form the whole structure.

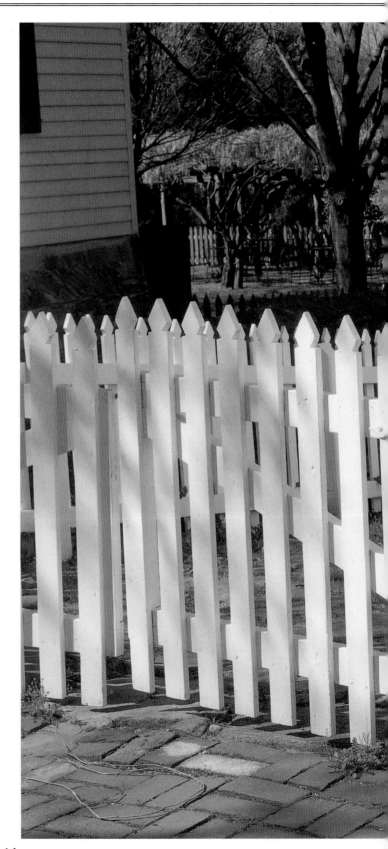

THE FOOTING

The footing is the foundation of the fence. Its purpose is to keep the framework firmly anchored in the earth, and secure from the seasonal effects of thaw and frost heave, which make it unstable and are likely to throw the fence out of alignment.

Typically, a footing is made up of several parts. The first is the postholes themselves, which are dug to a diameter appropriate to the posts, and to a depth consistent with the kind of post used and the soil type it's in. The second is the bed, consisting of crushed stone or gravel, which provides the post a place to rest and at the same time promotes drainage, which keeps water away from the wood. The final element is the filler material—concrete or earth—compacted around the posts once they're in position.

In the case of rail fences, there are no coverings involved, and the framework itself creates both the barrier and the look. Various methods of positioning and joining the frame components can be used to make the frame more attractive.

With the exception of jackleg or zigzag fences, which aren't buried in the earth, any framework consists of two parts. The posts are the vertical poles that hold the fence upright and connect it to the soil. The stringers, or rails, are the horizontal crosspieces that connect to the posts to complete the framework. It's important that the stringers be cut accurately so they can be joined to the posts in a secure manner, without gaps or misalignment.

THE FRAMEWORK

The framework is the skeleton, or structure, of the fence. With board fences, planks, panels, or pickets attach to the framework to provide a barrier or to create a certain look.

THE INFILL

The fence surface is called infill or siding, regardless of whether it's installed outside the framework, as in a picket or board fence, or within it, as panel or lath might be.

The range of materials available for infill is almost limitless, and your choice will affect the appearance of the fence considerably. Some kinds of infill are primarily aesthetic, while others offer a structural advantage in addition to a nice look.

COST AND MATERIALS ESTIMATES

Let's assume, at this point, that you already have a good idea of what you intend to accomplish. You've surveyed your site, gone through the planning steps outlined in Chapter Two, and roughed out a few sketches of the kind of fence you'd like to build.

If you're still in doubt about that last part, the fence styles illustrated in the next chapter and the examples shown in the gallery later on in the book will help. You can also spend a few afternoons walking or driving around local neighborhoods to examine how others have dealt with fences in their particular situations. Some may actually duplicate yours, which can save a lot of time in figuring out how to deal with knotty problems.

The point is, you'll need to have a detailed drawing or plan available—both to work from and to make cost and ordering estimates from. Here again, the use of graph paper will help you pin down exactly what you want by providing actual scale.

Sketch a single bay onto the paper as large as it will fit. If you let one inch equal one foot, an 8-½" X 11" sheet will

accommodate up to an 8'-tall by 10'-long bay in scale. More realistically, it will comfortably fit a scaled 5' by 8' bay and give you some room in the borders for notes and dimensions. Paper with a ¼" grid allows each square to represent 3", which shows enough detail to let you work with accuracy.

Be prepared to make quite a few drawings before you actually arrive at something you feel comfortable with. Also, keep in mind the practical aspects of this exercise by planning around the actual size of the materials you'll be working with. Treated 2 X 4s, for instance, are common and least expensive in 8' and 10' lengths, so you should make an effort to work in derivatives of those sizes to avoid waste.

As an example, pickets that measure 50" are too long to allow a pair to be cut from an 8' board, and too short to economically get two from a 10' board. 46" or 58" pickets, on the other hand, make good use of the lumber and allow a bit extra for trimming, besides. A similar approach can be taken with infill boards, panel material, and so forth.

Once you've completed your single-bay drawing, use it to make a detailed list of what you'll need in the way of materials. Organize the list by dimension so you'll be able to complete the order with a minimum of confusion, at least for the sake of the lumberyard clerk.

obstruction into the fence assembly; or routing the fence line around the obstruction completely.

If the obstacle is a tree, be aware that roots can easily be damaged by posts sunk in their midst, and the tree can die as a result. Better to reroute the fence or hold the posts away from the trunk slightly. Should a tree limb be the problem, you can frame an opening or notch in the fence structure to accommodate it, but be certain to leave enough clearance for inevitable growth.

Regardless of which method you choose, it will require that you calculate the materials needed to do it—either by removing them from the equation as appropriate or figuring on any additional supplies you might need.

Obstructions can also create problems with post spacing, which in a perfect world would be the same throughout the entire fence. Even such things as the end of a property line can be considered an obstruction, so sometimes post positions have to be compromised a bit.

If, for example, you planned on 8' bays and your fence line goes several feet beyond, you may have to change the spacing in that section of fence to absorb the extra distance in balance. Better, if possible, is to shorten the fence to lose the orphan (or lengthen it to add another full-size bay), or split whatever remains in half and add each to the end bays in that line of fence.

Set out the number and sizes of posts, stringers or rails, and any infill materials. Your design may require nailers or trim in addition to infill boards, and a cap or fascia of some kind if you're building an especially exquisite fence. Be sure to include all these elements in preparing your list. Then, simply multiply by the number of bays you intend to build to complete the order.

The result will, by the way, also allow you to calculate the cost of your fence, save for the incidental material costs for things such as hardware and fasteners (detailed in the previous chapter) and any concrete you might use in setting posts. It wouldn't be a bad idea to include a bit extra for unplanned circumstances, though, because it's not unlikely that you'll split a few boards or discover a warped post or two among your stock.

MANAGING OBSTRUCTIONS

It is possible—in fact, pretty likely—that you will be faced with some type of obstruction in plotting out your fence. It might be a tree or drain culvert, or perhaps a large rock or some feature you simply don't wish to move.

This can be dealt with by stopping the progress of the fence at that point and continuing again beyond it; integrating the

POSTHOLES AND FOOTINGS

The life and stability of your fence depend more on its footings than on any other factor. If you live in any but the most temperate areas of the country, you'll have to deal to some degree with frost heave, which is a phenomenon that occurs when water in the soil freezes, causing it to expand and "heave"—in the process forcing posts out of their holes and into misalignment.

In locations where the frost line is only a few inches beneath the surface, it's a fairly easy matter to dig beyond that point and sink the posts, which should be embedded at least 24" into the ground in any case. But in cold climates where the frost line can reach the 4' and 5' level, it is just impractical to purchase or even find 10' or longer posts to handle the job.

The cure? That depends on who you talk to. Some have had success with earth-and-gravel fill placed around posts to keep water from collecting in the vicinity. Others use concrete for the same purpose. Still others feel that they can control heave by nailing lateral anchors to the base of the posts or by boring $\frac{1}{2}$" holes through the wood, one perpendicular above another, and driving foot-long lengths of reinforcing bar through the openings.

Unfortunately, not one of these methods is absolutely guaranteed to work in every region of the country and in every type of soil. The best you can do is to seek the advice of one more experienced than yourself, which you can get from your local building inspector (for frost depths in your area) or a contractor who's familiar with the territory. Often, a fence-materials supplier can be a rich source of information, too.

It's obvious that a concrete post footing will cost more than one that uses earth-and-gravel backfill, but the greater expense does not necessarily mean a better result. That is proved over time by how it performs, which is another reason to speak with someone who has local experience when you can.

The soil-and-gravel fill method works best in stable soils, not in ones with a high clay content where they can slip, or in sandy, insecure earth where they are likely to move. If the fence is low or not under a lot of stress, even less-than-perfect soils may be able to hold a backfilled post satisfactorily.

With this method, the posthole diameter should be at least two times the width of the post overall, and the depth calculated by dividing the above-ground height of the post by 3 and adding another 4" to 6" for the gravel bed. For gate or end posts, go 12" deeper to ensure a solid ground connec-

POST FOOTINGS

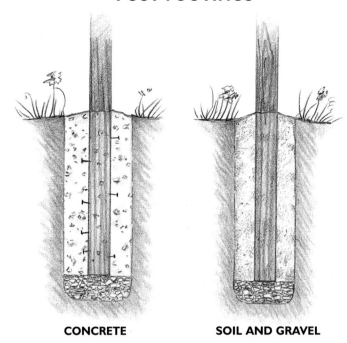

CONCRETE   **SOIL AND GRAVEL**

tion. Therefore, a 4 X 4 post rising 60" above grade level would require a hole 8" in diameter and at least 24" in depth.

The concrete-fill option will perform well in any kind of soil and is especially recommended for gate and end posts, or where a fence is subject to unusual stresses, such as a constant wind load against a tall, solid panel. While the increased diameter of the post assembly (the post and the concrete attached to it) multiplies the surface area actually bearing against the soil, it also protects the wood from the effects of moisture, providing the lower end is exposed to a bed of gravel at least 4" in depth.

With this approach, the hole diameter should be three times the width of the post, and the depth calculated by the same method used for a backfilled post. So, a 4 X 4 post rising 60" above the ground in this example would need a hole 12" in diameter and 24" to 36" deep, depending upon how it was used.

When figuring materials needs, remember to include the gravel base and concrete, if you use it. Each post base will require $\frac{1}{3}$ to $\frac{1}{2}$ cubic foot of $\frac{3}{4}$" gravel; another 1-$\frac{1}{2}$ cubic

feet will be needed for fill mix, or you can substitute that with an 80-lb. bag (⅔ cubic feet) of concrete premix if you prefer. Any anchoring materials—reinforcing bar, nails, or wooden cleats—need to be figured in as well.

WORKING WITH SLOPES

When the ground is not level, laying out a fence becomes a bit complicated. Sloped terrain brings with it a set of problems that have to be dealt with in both the planning and building stages.

A slope creates an angle that disturbs the perfect perpendicular environment of the fencebuilder. To right it, either the angle has to be straightened or the fence angled to conform. Before either one can occur, you need to establish how much of a slope you're dealing with.

Professionally, this is determined by an instrument known as a transit, which allows surveyors to set a level line and work in stages from it. You can gauge the rise and run of your slope in a more simple fashion by hammering a stake into

the ground at the terminal point of your intended fence at the high end and tying mason's line to it.

Then, run the line downhill to where you plan the fence to end and drive a tall stake at that point. By securing a line level to the string (or having a friend hold a regular level against the top of the line without distorting it) and pulling it taut against the stake, you can establish when the line is level and mark the stake at that point.

The rise is the vertical distance from the ground to the mark on the stake. The run is the horizontal distance between the stakes as measured along the level string. If the slope is especially steep, you may not be able to gauge it in one long stretch, but will have to take several short measurements and plot them together.

To transfer your actual measurements to graph paper for planning, just figure out a scale that will fit (if you let ¼" equal one foot, you can draw 40' of fence on an 11" sheet) and mark your run first. Then count up the number of squares to mark your rise on paper. Strike a line between the two points, and you have established the existing slope.

Some slopes will hardly be noticeable, while others can be quite severe. How you negotiate a grade change depends on your approach to the work, and the look you're after.

With a stepped framework, the fence frame remains square so all the joints are perpendicular. Each bay progresses up the slope by a measured amount, which remains constant over the duration of the slope.

To calculate that amount, you'll need to add up the number of bays in the length of the sloped section, then convert the rise from feet into inches, if not already. Divide the rise by the number of bays you have, and the result will be the number of inches that each bay must rise above the one below it in order for the fence to be evenly stepped. If these measurements are taken at the stringers, the infill will automatically be located in the correct position.

Stepped frames are ideal for moderate, even slopes and will accommodate board or picket infill as well as panel materials, which can be mounted to nailers inset within the

STEPPED FRAME

framework. They can also be worked up as rail fencing. Once completed, a stepped-frame fence has a planned and somewhat formal look to it that suggests an architectural influence. Because the fence is rectilinear and stands separate from the ground, triangular gaps occur at the bottom.

To avoid that, a modification can be made to the infill, if desired, after the framework is complete. Rather than allowing it to conform to the rectilinear pattern of each bay, it can be installed to follow the contour of grade, both at the bottom and the top of the fence. The result is that the infill extends past the upper stringers on each bay's high side and the lower stringers on the down side, filling the triangular

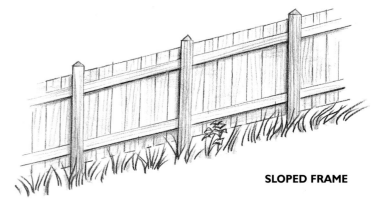

SLOPED FRAME

gaps mentioned earlier. This treatment only works with nailed-on infill (not inset panels), and works best when the grade is rather steep.

Sloping frames are built to follow the contour of the ground. With this style, the posts remain upright, but the stringers are mounted at an angle to match the grade. The stringer ends must be cut at a complementary angle to assure a proper fit, and if dadoes are used, they must be cut into the posts at angle as well.

Any type of surface-mounted infill will work with this construction...but panel materials or anything that needs to be inset would be difficult to custom-fit to every opening. The sloped framework method is suitable for most any type of grade and works well on uneven ground because it can be adjusted as the fence progresses.

For a more finished look, the lower and upper edges of the infill boards are usually trimmed to run parallel with the angle of the stringers. However, it's possible to devise a distinctive appearance (and incidentally save some trimming

STEPPED BOARDS

time) by mounting the boards themselves in step fashion individually along the sloping framework. If the corners are held in a straight line, the fence will not have an unfinished look even though there will be gaps at the ground.

PLOTTING YOUR LAYOUT

The time has come to transfer the marks you've made on paper to actual points in the ground. This is done with the use of batter boards and mason's line, which will be set up to indicate the centerline of the fence along its length.

Batter boards are simply sharpened 2 X 4s driven into the ground that support horizontal braces; these allow the string line to be adjusted incrementally right or left to straighten alignment or to make a perfect right angle when needed.

To assure that the lines truly represent what you drew on paper, it's important to follow these steps closely:

1.   Cut a fair supply of 1 X 4s or 2 X 4s to about 24" in length and sharpen one end of each with a hatchet. Cut another supply to 20" in length and leave the ends square. You'll need two sharpened stakes and one cross brace for each location that indicates an end post or a change in grade from level. Each corner or change in direction requires two sets of boards.

2.   Drive a pair of stakes 18" apart into the ground about 3' beyond what is to be the terminal points of each run of fence line. Sink them 10" or 12" into the soil. If one of the fence runs begins at an existing fence or at a wall foundation, drive the stakes as close as possible to it.

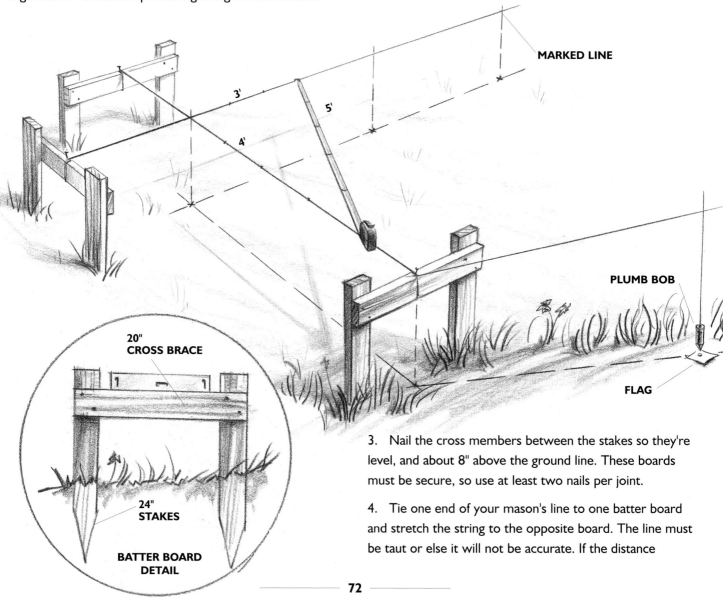

MARKED LINE

3'

5'

4'

PLUMB BOB

FLAG

20" CROSS BRACE

24" STAKES

BATTER BOARD DETAIL

3.   Nail the cross members between the stakes so they're level, and about 8" above the ground line. These boards must be secure, so use at least two nails per joint.

4.   Tie one end of your mason's line to one batter board and stretch the string to the opposite board. The line must be taut or else it will not be accurate. If the distance

To plot a symmetrical curve in your fence line, you'll need five stakes (the ones cut for the batter boards will do), a steel rod, and the two reference points from which you'll be establishing the curve. If existing fence posts are your reference points, you'll need only three stakes.

Stretch a line between the two points of the curve you wish to make, then measure to find the halfway point of the line. Mark it with one of the stakes. Tie another line to this center stake and pull it back, away from the curve side, to a distance about equal to that of the first line. Drive a stake at that point, and tighten the line around it. This line must be perpendicular to the first, and can be checked using the 3-4-5 method described in Step 5.

Drive the last stake into the ground at some point along the second line and loop a third line around it. Stretch the end of this line to one of the end points of the curve. The shorter the line, the steeper the arc will be; to create a shallower arc, move the pivot stake farther from the fence line. Tie a steel rod to the free end of the pivot line and use it to scrape a track in the earth from one end of the fence post line to the other. Then measure along the arc and mark to place the posts.

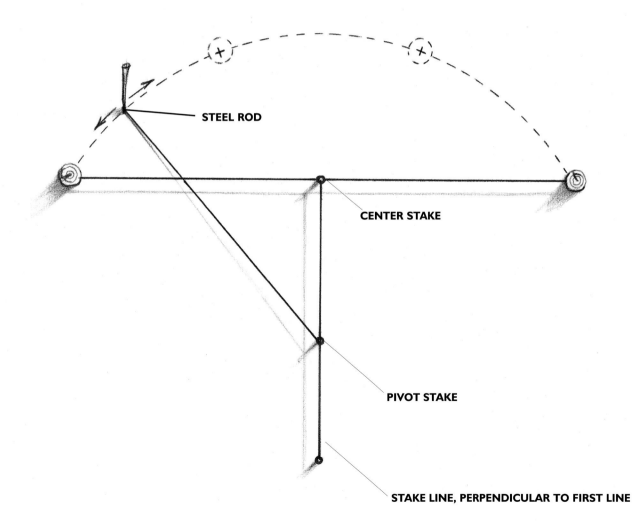

STEEL ROD

CENTER STAKE

PIVOT STAKE

STAKE LINE, PERPENDICULAR TO FIRST LINE

between the boards is so great that the string sags, you'll have to drive in a center batter board and stretch two separate lines outward to connect to the end boards.

Any obstructions in the path of the line should be removed. Bushes can be tied back, and low shrubbery or rocks can be avoided by making the batter board stakes taller. At grade changes, where you've established batter boards to take the line up or down a slope, you'll need to eye the string from the last point to make sure it's in alignment with the string already in place.

5. Make lateral adjustments on the lines as needed. After you've established that the placement of the string represents the plan you laid out beforehand, measure to see that the lines are even with walkways, walls, and any other reference points you may have planned against. At corners, check for perpendicular by either laying a square against the string, or even better, employing the contractor's 3-4-5 measuring technique. To do this, mark a point 3' from the corner on one leg and 4' from it on the other leg; measure the distance between those two points to confirm a measurement of 5'. If it's more or less than that, adjust the strings right or left on the batter boards as needed to achieve the 5' measurement.

MARKING
THE POST HOLES

On level ground, or sloped or rolling terrain, evenly spaced fence posts make the statement that the structure was planned and built with care. From a more practical point of view, they all but guarantee that parts such as stringers and pickets can be cut to consistent lengths and widths without special fitting on the job.

Marking the hole locations is a simple job, but it must be done carefully. You'll carry marks on the stretched line down to positions on the ground through the use of a plumb bob, described in Chapter Three. Then you'll dig the postholes exactly at the locations marked. Follow these steps as described:

1. Verify your plan one more time by walking the lines. Measure the distance between the end points at each batter board to see if they equal the distances you had written

down. Keep in mind that it's not the overall length that matters as much as it is how the post spacing will work out; check by dividing the overall distance by the total number of posts minus one. The posts should be evenly spaced as figured, unless you made an adjustment to compensate earlier on.

2. Measure off your posthole locations and mark them on the stretched line. The postholes are to be marked on center, or from the center of one post to the center of the one adjacent. Begin at the intersection of two lines (a corner) and use a tape to confirm the desired distances. Mark right on the string with a felt marker, or use narrow strips of duct tape to indicate the positions.

3. Transfer the string positions to points on the ground using the plumb bob. To do this, hold the plumb bob's string against the mark on the stretched line and let the suspended bob point indicate the spot directly below. Mark each one with a nail stuck through a small scrap of plastic or cloth. These are called flags, and the procedure is referred to as "flagging the holes."

On slopes or inclines, the string's angle will throw off the spacing, so you cannot measure along the string. Instead, drive a temporary rod upright at the last level flag and measure one bay width to the angled string. When the measuring tape is level, mark the string, and repeat the procedure along the slope as needed. Then suspend the plumb bob and position the flags as before.

Mark the batter board string positions and loosen the line to make it easier to excavate the postholes.

4. Dig each posthole exactly at the center of the flagged points, using the guidelines outlined earlier. The idea is to cut the sides of the holes plumb and clean, which is surprisingly easy with a clamshell digger, even though the work itself is difficult. Leave the excavated earth near the holes, for you'll need it for fill later. If you're setting the posts in concrete, shovel the earth into a wheelbarrow and use it elsewhere. Set a gravel bed into each of the holes.

SETTING THE POSTS

There's little question that setting the fence posts is the proof of your work. For no matter how well-positioned the

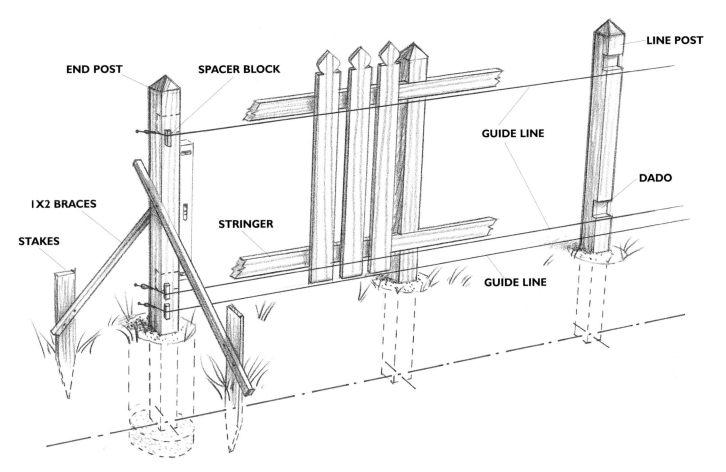

END POST

SPACER BLOCK

LINE POST

GUIDE LINE

DADO

1 X 2 BRACES

STRINGER

STAKES

GUIDE LINE

holes are, if you're careless in aligning and plumbing the posts within those holes, the pieces won't fit together and the fence line will appear crooked and shoddily built.

If your fence plan includes precut dadoes for the stringers or uses mortised posts to secure the rails, you'll need to set the posts at exactly the right height. If you'll be nailing the stringers on later, the height isn't critical because you'll be trimming the tops after the posts are set. And, very important—posts with precut open mortises such as the kind used with split-rail fencing cannot be set all at once. Rather, each bay must be assembled before the next rail set and post is installed because the rails are too long to fit into the openings otherwise.

SET THE POSTS IN THIS ORDER:

1. Reposition the lines on the batter boards so they'll be touching the outside edge of the posts. To calculate this, measure the thickness of a post and halve that dimension. Then slide the strings over from their earlier marked points by that amount. Pull the lines taut and tie them off.

2. Place the end posts in each section of fence. If you're planning to use cleats or reinforcing bar for additional anchoring, now's the time to get them in place. These posts will be the terminals from which the line posts are measured. Tamp the posts into their gravel beds. If the posts are dadoed, measure the distance from the tops to grade level, and make them equal by cutting from the bottom of one of the posts. Install two 1 X 2 braces on adjacent flats of the posts and plumb them, one at a time. Hold the post exactly upright and flush to the line, then have a helper drive a stake next to the lower end of each brace. Nail the braces to the stakes, then go on to repeat the procedure for the opposite end post.

3. Stretch another line between the two end posts about 12" from the top. Tie the line to a small nail in the end face of one post and pull it to the opposite post, then tie it off on a second nail after leveling the line. If you're mounting stringers flush with the post faces and need clearance for picket adjustments later on, set the line off on spacer blocks (as shown in the illustration) equal to

the thickness of the pickets. At this point, you can place the line posts into the holes you've prepared, tamping and aligning them as you did the end posts, but this time with both the upper and lower strings. Once they're braced, you're ready to set them permanently. Again, if you're setting dadoed posts, measure from the top and remove any extra from the bottom if needed. Refer to Chapter Ten for more detail on an actual project.

4. Back-fill or pour concrete into the holes to secure the posts forever. If using backfill and gravel, pour in a half-foot or so, then tamp vigorously around the circumference of the post with a steel bar or 2 X 2 before adding more fill. Tamp again, then repeat until there's enough fill to form a sloped collar around the post, which will help to shed rain. If you choose to go with concrete fill, mix the prepared blend according to instructions (it should be stiff and formable, but do not touch it with your bare hands, as it'll burn the skin). Then shovel the mix into the holes one at a time, and "rod" the mixture by moving a steel bar up and down within it to remove any air bubbles. Form a sloped cap with a trowel or putty knife. Do not remove the post bracing immediately, as the concrete needs several days to cure. If you can work around the braces, there's no hurry to remove them in any case.

INSTALLING
THE STRINGERS

Before you install the stringers, you should mark the posts for cutting height, unless they've already been pre-set. The tops should be cut square if a cap board is to be installed, or stepped frames are being used. They'll be cut at an angle if a sloped framework is used, or if a point or slope is desired at the top of each post. It's not really practical to cut anything complicated on site, so it's best to plan that kind of work for the shop beforehand.

Follow these steps to trim the post tops and install the stringers:

1. Mark the tops of the posts by stretching a line between a small nail driven into one end post at the desired height and another nail driven into the post at the opposite end. Measure up from the ground to check height on sloped ter-

rain, and use a line level on flat ground. Draw a pencil line at each line post where the string crosses it.

2. Carry the lines around the posts to the other three sides as required. For simple square cuts, use the blade of a combination square to "walk" the mark straight around the post. For angled cuts, a square can be used to carry the upper and lower straight lines, while a sliding bevel is used to copy the angle and recreate it on the opposite face.

3. Cut the posts to height with a crosscut saw or a circular saw. With the power saw, you can use the edge of a square to guide the shoe of the saw for an accurate cut. With a handsaw, make your initial cut deep and true, then follow the line faithfully. The work is more comfortable and accurate if you can set up a ladder to position yourself at the right height. If you haven't yet removed the post bracing, do it now.

4. Measure for the stringer positions from the top of the posts down. On level ground and straight slopes, it's easy to place the stringer position marks in pencil on the end posts and stretch a line between nails driven at those marks. Stepped framework and sections of fence covering uneven ground will have to be measured and marked individually. Carry the marks to the line posts where the strings cross, in any case.

5. Measure the top stringer spans for fit and cut the stringers to length. A ¾" steel tape will do a noble job if held straight, exactly at the place where the stringer is to go, whether it's on the face of, or in between, the posts. Transfer the measurement to the board and mark. Use a square and pencil to strike the mark full-width, then cut the stringer just to the outside of the line. Nail (or screw) the stringer in place, using at least two fasteners per joint (see the joint details later in this chapter). Repeat the procedure with each successive span. Do not cut all the stringers first and then try to install them, or you'll discover that the posts have most likely moved slightly with nailing.

6. Measure the bottom spans for fit and cut and mount the lower stringers, using the same procedure. Though it's less likely that the posts will shift at this point, it's still a good idea to work your way down the line progressively.

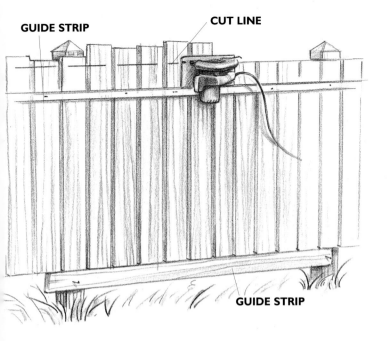

GUIDE STRIP　　　CUT LINE

GUIDE STRIP

PLACING THE INFILL

At this point, you are aware that there are two types of infill treatments: surface mounted and inset. If you're building a rail-style fence, you're acutely aware that your work is now complete, since it doesn't require any infill.

Surface-mounted infills are by far the most popular for the home builder because they generally use less material, are less expensive, and are not as complicated to construct. In their simplest form, square-ended boards are nailed to the surface of the stringers with only the bottom ends held level. The tops are cut to a marked line later. More involved surface treatments use repeating patterns, or styled pickets (see Chapter Eight) that may be arranged in a certain profile.

There are a number of ways to install surface-mounted infill, and the following is typical.

1. Drive a small nail 3" above the ground into one end post. Tie a line and stretch it to the opposite post. Check for level and tie the line off on a second nail at that point. This will be your guideline for the bottom edge of the infill boards. Another option is to tack an 8' 1 X 4 between the posts of each bay to serve as a guide strip. If you want less

clearance to the ground, you can always rip the board down slightly.

2. Begin at one end of a bay and position the first board by setting it to the string or strip, then check for plumb with a level. Nail or screw the board to the top and bottom stringers, using two fasteners per joint. If the boards are particularly wide, you can use three, but don't migrate too closely to the edge of the wood or it may split.

3. Place the second board against the first and check for plumb before fastening. If you're installing pickets or setting flat boards with an intentional gap, you can make a spacer board by ripping a plank-length strip to the space width you require, then screwing a small block at one end to serve as a hanger cleat. Place the spacer against the just-installed board and let it hang from the top stringer. Then push the board to be installed against the spacer, and simply remove it once the second board is secured. Continue until the section is completed.

4. Measure from the lower edge up at each end of the fence section to establish the cutoff line along the top edge. Then measure the distance from the left edge of your circular saw's shoe to the blade, and tack a straight strip of wood to the fence boards so its edge is that distance from the cutoff line. Set the depth of the blade to cut through the boards but do not allow it to contact the posts, as it will leave a kerf mark. Repeat on the subsequent bays.

5. Remove the upper and lower guide strips from the fence boards and clear away any remaining string.

Inset treatments take more time to build but look more formal and show the same face on both sides. Here are the basic steps to completion.

1. Measure the framed opening of each bay separately and record height and width. Check to see if the bays are square by placing a framing square in two opposite corners.

2. Cut the infill material to length for the first bay. If (especially for panels) the opening isn't quite square, you can cheat a bit as any gaps will be hidden behind the nailers. Cut the vertical and horizontal 1 X 2 nailers to length as well. The ends can be either mitered for clean corners or simply

CLEATED JOINT

MORTISED JOINT

butted, with the horizontal strips running full length. If you plan on routing a bead or special shape into the nailer strips, do it now. You can also change the dimension of the strips if you care to.

3. Use a marking gauge to scribe a centerline at several points in the middle of the frame face. Then measure from one edge of the frame to place the nailers one-half the width of the infill material from the centerline. Fasten the one set of nailers to the frame as a perimeter, using finish nails spaced 9" to 12" apart.

4. Toenail the infill panels or boards to the frame, working from left to right. On a vertical pattern, check for plumb on individual boards before you secure them. Use two nails per board.

5. Nail the remaining set of nailers to the frame on the opposite side of the infill to dress the exposed edges. Repeat the entire procedure with the remaining fence bays.

JOINTS NAILED, AND NOT

It may come as a surprise that not all joints have to be nailed, or, more accurately, fastened. Some can be simply fitted together, and others may be a combination of wood joinery and sound fastenry.

There's not as much mystery to screws because we can see how they work, with points and deep threads. But a nail is different. Actually, when a nail is driven into a piece of wood, the point wedges the fibers apart and allows the shank of the nail to pass through. Once it's sunk, the fibers squeeze back against the nail shank, and friction keeps the nail from backing out of the wood. As lumber thickness increases, the nail's ability to resist withdrawal and snapping increases as well, because there's more wood to support it.

In hard and dense woods, it helps to drill a pilot hole—a small opening perhaps 50% to 75% of the nail's diameter—to guide the nail and keep the wood from splitting. In soft

SPLINE JOINT

DADOED JOINT

woods, blunting the nail point will also keep the wood from splitting but will also reduce its ability to stay put. Too large a diameter nail will almost always cause a split to occur, even if the wood isn't prone to it.

When toenailing—driving a nail at a 45-degree angle to join a stringer to a post, for example—it's not always convenient to drill a pilot hole first. Instead, start the nails at the proper angle about 1" from the end of the wood before setting it in position. Placing the board on a solid surface will allow you to drive the nails far enough in that just the points protrude, and they will catch on the nailed surface.

A simple **butted joint** is the weakest example of a wooden union. Usually, a joint's strength can be increased by cutting a different surface into it. This can be as simple as a **beveled** edge, or more complicated, as a **half-** or **end-lap** joint. The increased surface area exposed to the mating pieces works to strengthen the bond and keep it from moving.

A **notch** is a V-groove cut into the surface of the wood. A **dado** is a rectangular notch cut partially into the surface of a wooden member to accept another piece of wood. These are measured against the piece that's to fit and cut accordingly. The waste wood is removed with a chisel after several saw cuts are made through it.

A **mortise** is a socket cut into a post to house a rail or other wooden part. Fence mortises can be through (open at both ends) or blind (open at only one end).

A **cleat** is a strip of wood nailed beneath a board to help support it in addition to fasteners.

The examples that follow will help to clarify the various ways of joining fence components successfully.

JOINING FENCE COMPONENTS

An endlap joint used to secure the cap rail of a post-and-board fence. The ends are cut to overlap each other by 1", using a circular saw set to cut half the thickness of the board, or $3/4$", in repeated passes. Waste is removed with a chisel. Four nails hold the joint in place, and they're driven toward the center at a slight angle because end grain does not hold a nail particularly well.

A simple butt joint in the same circumstances as the end-lapped post-and-board cap. Though it's true that this joint is easy to make, it's also one of the least able to resist stress from warpage and movement.

A miter joint used on the cap rail at the corner post. This construction is similar to the butt joint on the post-and-board cap noted previously, but applied to a right angle.

The cap rail on this faux infill fence has been given a $3/8$" X $7/8$" dado on the table saw. The groove keeps the infill boards in position as long as the cap remains nailed securely to the post. A design such as this would be prone to warpage at the top and bottom rails.

A dado holds rail members firmly and provides a finished, professional look. The shoulder cuts and a series of center cuts are made from the surface using a circular saw. Then the waste is removed to a consistent depth with a mortise chisel. The rails can be nailed or screwed in place.

On rail boards, butt joints are staggered so they don't fall in line with each other adjacently at the same post. Typically, a 16' board spans three posts. On a round post such as this, two nails per end are used; otherwise, three nails would provide more holding power on a flat bearing surface.

A beveled joint allows for expansion and contraction without leaving a conspicuous gap. It's also far less complicated to cut than a half-lap joint.

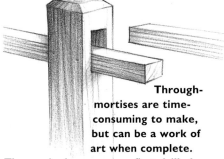

Through-mortises are time-consuming to make, but can be a work of art when complete. The marked corners are first drilled through with a small spade bit, then connected along each shoulder and seat with a series of bores. The post is drilled from both faces to keep the wood from splitting. Waste is removed, and the inside surfaces cleaned up, with a chisel.

These cleats are nailed to the post to provide support for stringers mounted on-flat. After the cleats are in place, the stringers are toenailed to the post.

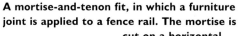

A mortise-and-tenon fit, in which a furniture joint is applied to a fence rail. The mortise is cut on a horizontal, and the rail is trimmed to create a square-shouldered tenon. The mortise goes all the way through.

Dadoes can be cut into the inner post faces as well. Here, measurement is important because if the dadoes are cut too deeply, the post's strength is compromised.

A basic toenailed butt joint used to fasten between-post stringers. Decking screws can be used in place of nails for a more positive connection.

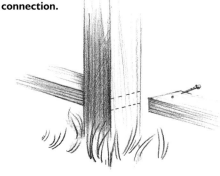

Notches can be cut to hold stringers in place and to keep them from migrating. Nails are used in addition. In this example, the flat-to-the-bottom cut provides good support but collects water; when the angled cut is placed at the bottom, it provides an avenue for escape yet still keeps the stringer secured.

Typical joint construction for cedar, larch, locust, and pine split-rail fencing. These are manufacturer-cut joints that can be duplicated by the do-it-yourselfer if desired. Precise workmanship is not needed and in fact would detract from the joint's ambiance.

FENCE ADDITIONS AND REPAIRS

Often, a fence can be added onto simply by carrying the same construction method beyond an end post. To make a good job of it, you need to make an accurate assessment of the kind of stock used in the existing fence—posts, stringers, infill, trim, and caps if any. The bay dimensions have to be repeated faithfully, and the new section aligned with the old by stringing a mason's line from the existing section to the new terminal point.

If you want to change direction, tie into an existing end post and proceed just as if you were building a new fence. It's a good idea to survey the fence, or check its structural condition, before proceeding with any additions because repairs may have to be made first.

To brace a sagging post, the simplest method is to excavate in front of it to create a second post hole. Then a short cripple post—extending perhaps 3' above ground and 3' below—can be set into the hole using the same techniques described earlier in this chapter. Once plumbed and fixed flush against the old post, it can be lag-screwed to hold the existing post in place. The top should be beveled to shed water.

If placing a cripple post would be too conspicuous, you'll have to install a post mid-span in the sagging section. Clear any growth from the area and dig your post hole as before, and prepare it with a gravel bed. Then cut a full-length post of the same dimension as the ones existing and set it upright alongside the fence to mark the places where it might meet stringers or other structural elements. Cut half-lap joints into both the stringers and the post to allow the pieces to join with faces flush, using fasteners as required. Trim the top as needed. Plumb and brace the post and bay, and fill the hole with concrete for permanent support. Remove the bracing after two or three days.

Occasionally, you'll need to pull a post to replace it completely. This is difficult on a board fence, but common with post-and-rail or wire-fence construction. Two simple methods work. The first is to use your pry bar or a pipe as a

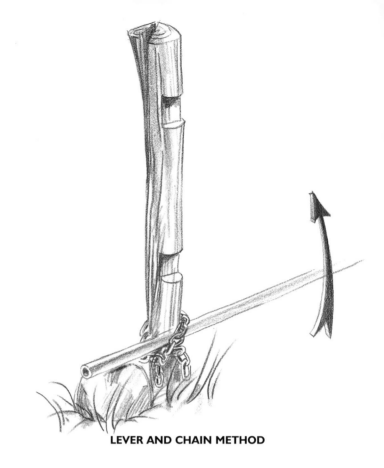

LEVER AND CHAIN METHOD

lever by chaining it to the post and tightening the chain with a bolt passed through the end links. Let the lever extend a foot or so beyond the post and place a rock or block of concrete beneath it. Pull up on the lever while simultaneously wiggling the post back and forth; it should come up in degrees, and you can slide the chain downward as needed until the post is free.

You can also make a post-puller by welding a 2" X 4" U-bracket to a 12" section of 2" X 2" tubular steel. A metal plate welded to the bottom provides a foot for support. A 1-3/4" pipe section 6' to 8' long is bolted into the bracket 12" from one end so it can pivot up and down. By welding a C-clamp (or even a length of chain) to the end, the post can be gripped and the stand provides a ready fulcrum for the lever as it's pushed downward.

For steel fence posts, replace the chain or clamp with a 1/4" steel plate cut to include a notch slightly larger than the posts being removed. One leg of the notch catches in a lug as the lever is worked, raising the post.

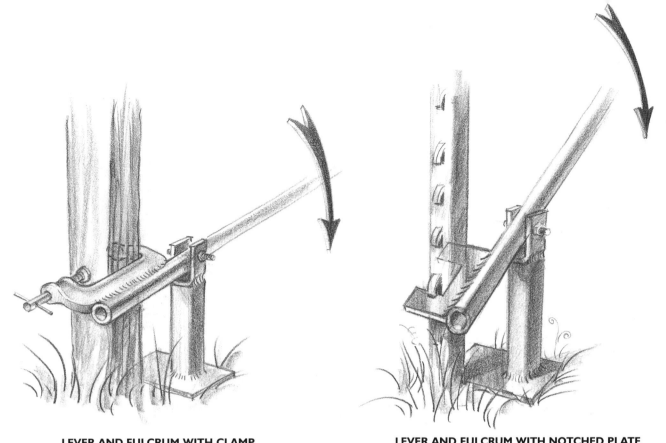

LEVER AND FULCRUM WITH CLAMP

LEVER AND FULCRUM WITH NOTCHED PLATE

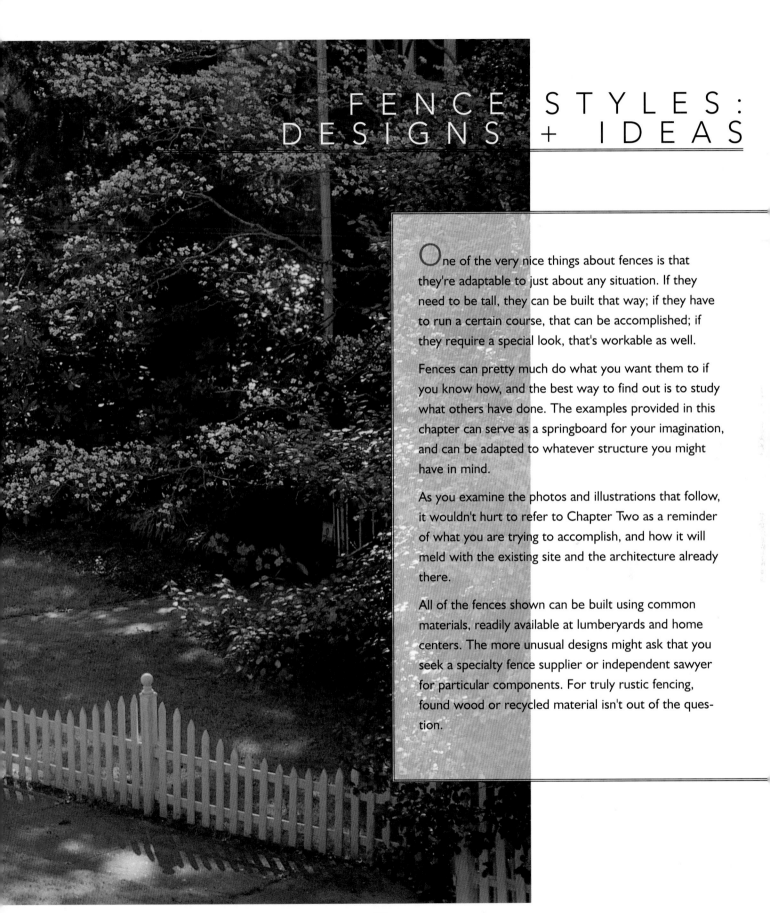

FENCE STYLES:
DESIGNS + IDEAS

One of the very nice things about fences is that they're adaptable to just about any situation. If they need to be tall, they can be built that way; if they have to run a certain course, that can be accomplished; if they require a special look, that's workable as well.

Fences can pretty much do what you want them to if you know how, and the best way to find out is to study what others have done. The examples provided in this chapter can serve as a springboard for your imagination, and can be adapted to whatever structure you might have in mind.

As you examine the photos and illustrations that follow, it wouldn't hurt to refer to Chapter Two as a reminder of what you are trying to accomplish, and how it will meld with the existing site and the architecture already there.

All of the fences shown can be built using common materials, readily available at lumberyards and home centers. The more unusual designs might ask that you seek a specialty fence supplier or independent sawyer for particular components. For truly rustic fencing, found wood or recycled material isn't out of the question.

THE PICKET FENCE

It's classic and traditional, and if you were to choose one style that would least likely clash with any site, the picket would have to be it; it's easily the safest choice.

It's also a fence that's fun to work with because there are so many design variables. Pickets and posts offer countless opportunities for expressing yourself and your particular tastes and fancies in the shapes of their tops and finials.

Picket-style fences tend to be lower than many others to create a physical, but not a visual, barrier. A 3' to 4-½' height is not intimidating and encourages conversation over the fence. Posts are set on narrower centers than usual, too, so the height-to-width ratios remain favorable.

A post size of 4 X 4 is common; 6 X 6s are used less frequently and fit better with a taller, more formal picket treatment. Rails, in general, are 2 X 4s fastened on flat, though

there are plenty of on-edge examples to be seen. For pickets, the most common choices are 1 X 3s or 1 X 4s, spaced between 2-½" and 3" apart. Sometimes, pickets made of slat materials—thinner and narrower than that just described—are used to create a period effect.

Precut pickets aren't generally available; the trend is more toward preassembled 3-½' X 8' fence sections rather than component parts. To get anything other than square-end pickets, then, you'll probably have to design and cut them yourself.

A handful of examples are shown here. The best way to approach the job is to draw a full-scale image of the shape you desire on a piece of paper, then trace and cut it into a ¼" hardboard template with a coping saw or a fine-toothed jigsaw blade. Prepare to go through a lot of scrap before you get it just right. Depending upon the design, several cutting options are open.

Simple curved lines or oblique angles can be cut with a jigsaw. So long as there are no curves involved, angles alone (whether two-sided or crosswise slices) can be cut with a circular saw or a radial-arm saw if you have access to one. Small-diameter (½" to 1-½") through-holes can be made with a hole saw or a spade bit, and convex curves of any size are easily fashioned with the appropriate-diameter hole saw.

FENCE PICKET STYLES

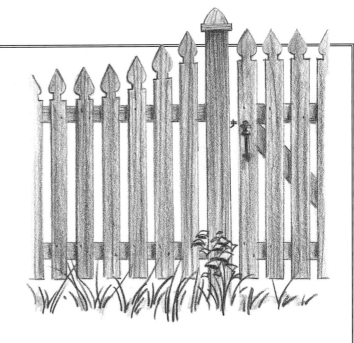

DIAMOND

SPADE

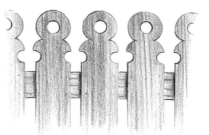

EYE AND IRIS

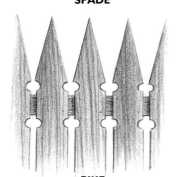

PIKE

OBLIQUE

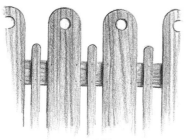

EYE

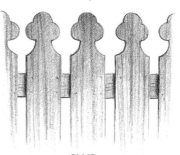

CLUB

FENCE POST STYLES

ROUTED AND CUT FINIAL

MITERED TRIM MOLDING

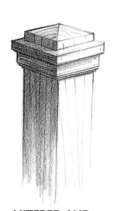

MITERED AND ROUNDOVER MOLDING

FINIAL AND CHAMFERED EDGE

CUT TOP AND VEINS

Professionals "gang-cut" pickets because it's quicker than shaping them individually and far more accurate. Gang-cutting means to stack and clamp several together, and cut them as one. For the home-shop hobbyist, that translates into simply clamping two pickets together to a stable work surface with a C-clamp so they extend past any interference, and making the shapes desired. 1-½" is a reasonable amount of wood for a jigsaw or hole saw to work through, and any sanding can be done with the clamps still in place.

Post designs are not all easy to make. Simple slant-cut tops or four-faced points (see the style detailed in Chapter Ten) can be trimmed without a lot of detail work. But true finials-the decorative knobs and such that you see on Victorian-era fencing—require lathes and other woodworking equipment that many people don't have.

Given the situation, there are three options: One, purchase the decorative embellishments from an architectural supply house (listed in the advertising sections of better wood-working magazines) or a local millwork shop and fasten them to your posts; two, invest in a lathe and spend some time learning how to use it; three, use trim and kerf-cuts in a creative way to make up for the lack of difficult ornamentation.

Examples of the latter are shown in some of the accompanying illustrations. Miter-cut 1 X 1s and trim moldings can be fit and finish-nailed around posts that have had their tops cut with common woodworking tools; a chamfered edge

can be routed into four corners the length of the post save for a 1-¼" stop at the top and bottom; and ¼"-deep saw kerfs can create decorative veins in an otherwise pedestrian post.

THE BOARD FENCE

Board fences tend to be built for a purpose, then designed to fit the situation. They make good privacy fences and windbreaks, and offer more security than many open styles of wood fence.

Because they require a good deal of lumber to build, board fences are costly. Furthermore, they can be adapted in many ways to create almost limitless impressions and can be hybridized with other style features as well. They tend to be taller than picket fences, up to 6' or 7' in some cases, but are narrower by proportion, with bays usually 8' in width. It's important that the posts be well anchored or buried 3' into the ground, for these fences are weighty and prone to the effects of wind, since they block it so effectively.

The fence framework is straightforward and uncomplicated since it is not meant to show. 4 X 4 posts and 2 X 4 stringers on flat are all that's required, with no fancy mortise or dado work. Simple butt joints are adequate.

The designs are varied. In its most basic form, a board fence has squared, flat-cut tops. Other designs include points, spade tips, and flat tops with miter-cut sides. Wide 12" fence boards can have random-width picket tops cut

into them, or alternate-width boards—1 X 4s and 1 X 8s—can be mounted in a recurring pattern.

Both horizontal and vertical board-and-batten arrangements are possible (using 1 X 6 boards and 1 X 2 battens), as is a butted-edge diagonal pattern. Even beveled siding has successfully been used, with vertical studs nailed between the stringers to help support the boards midspan.

Other variations include vertical 1 X 8s alternately placed on opposite sides of the fence and, similarly, placed alternately by bays rather than individually (a sensible way of presenting an equal view no matter which side of the fence is observed). Another treatment with the same result is the "faux infill" approach (see page 80) in which the boards are inset within a channel dadoed into the rails.

For hybrid fencing, a third stringer is added at the 4' or 5' level and the opening filled with lattice panel, bamboo, welded wire (for vines), or some type of picket treatment.

THE PANEL FENCE

Panel fences are really just outdoor screens, built either for total privacy (if solid), or as a windbreak, or an exterior win-

dow (if glassed). Depending upon the material used as the inset, they can be moderately to extremely expensive to erect.

By their very nature, panel fences are tall, extending 4-½' to 6' above the ground and 3' into it so the posts are well anchored. The panels can be made of many materials, though plywood, glass, hardboard, and fiberglass are most common. Plywood is especially versatile because it comes in a variety of patterns and textures.

Fence posts are 4 X 4s or 6 X 6s, which are broad enough across their face to accommodate 2 X 4 stringers (to support the panels) and 1 X 1 nailer strips (to keep the panels in place). In some designs, stiff ¾" plywood can be nailed directly to the face of the posts rather than being inset, and the butted joints covered with 1-bys. A broad 2 X 6 cap then covers the end grain of the posts and panels to prevent exposure to moisture.

Since panel goods come in 4' X 8' dimensions, the fence bays are designed around that size, broken horizontally with a stringer to fit a narrower panel at the top or bottom if the fence is over 4-½' tall.

Panel fences tend to be formal and even elegant because they're customarily used to enclose patios and quiet, private areas around the house, and so must tie into it architecturally. This is one fence that you'd be well advised to research thoroughly before beginning any construction.

THE WATTLE + WOVEN FENCE

One of the most attractive and surprisingly easy-to-accomplish fence projects is the woven fence, which has its roots in our earliest agrarian experiences. It is nothing more than a series of thin wooden strips arranged as in a basket weave around more substantial posts or rails.

In its simplest configuration, it's known as the wattle fence, a ubiquitous presence in British meadows and pastures long before Colonial settlement. The wattle's practical beauty is in its use of shallow-driven posts, which—in the days before augers and posthole diggers—made it a popular item indeed. Long twigs and supple branches are woven horizon-

tally between 3" posts, which are spaced perhaps four feet apart. These laterals can be tightly stacked to create a dense and impervious barrier, or set loosely to make a more open and inviting structure. The wattle's tall posts do not occur by accident—as the wood in contact with the ground decays with age, the posts can be driven farther into the earth and new wattle added on top.

A variation on this venerable design is appropriate to cottages and rustic settings. The woven lath fence is a more structured, and vertical, treatment of the old wattle theme. It is fashioned from 4' sections of wood lath (thin boards perhaps 1-½" wide and only 3/16" to ¼" thick) woven between three horizontal 2 X 3 rails fastened between 4 X 4 posts spaced 8' apart. The beauty of this fence comes not only from its rustic charm, but in the fact that it doesn't require perfection—it asks only that the posts be square and upright, and the rails securely fastened to them. The lath does the rest; its spacing is not as discretionary as that of the wattle, since the lath isn't actually fastened to the rails, but relies on friction against them and against the adjacent

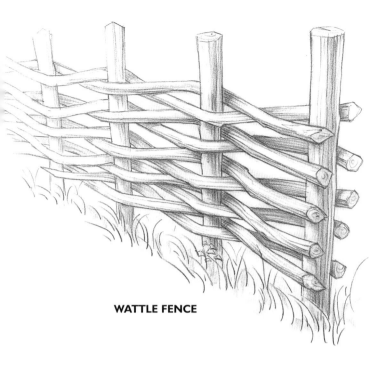

WATTLE FENCE

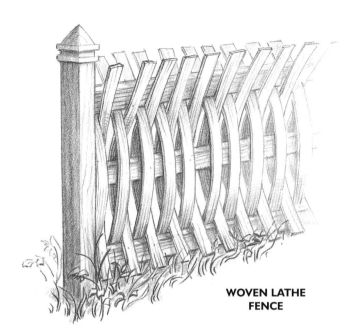

**WOVEN LATHE
FENCE**

pieces to provide the necessary support.

The basket-weave fence is a more substantial and suburban approach, yet still evolved from the earliest woven fences. Each section is an eight-foot panel built between two 4 X 4s. The woven laterals are comprised of long lath, or bender board, anchored between vertical nailer strips fastened to the posts. A 1 X 3 upright spacer at midbay provides the "wave" that makes the fence a woven structure. Two by fours fastened on top of and between the posts cap the upper and lower edges of each bay.

An authentic restoration of a woven withe fence of saplings at Plymouth Colony, Massachusetts.

THE POST-AND-BOARD FENCE

This is the fence seen in rural areas, used to enclose large tracts of land. The fact that it's also known as "horse fence" evinces its reputation as a sturdy, quickly erected, and—by

the way—comparatively inexpensive way to contain acreage. Because post-and-board styles use considerably less lumber than many more decorative fences (yet aren't as stark as a basic post-and-wire enclosure) they tend to be a wise choice, economically, for those faced with the task of wrapping up a few acres.

Characteristically, the post-and-board fence is 4' high with three 1 X 6 rails spanning 8', 4 X 4 square or round post centers. For larger livestock, the post height is increased to 5' or more, dimension to 6 X 6, and 2 X 6s may be used. For smaller stock, more rails can be added or spacing can be altered to make it difficult for the animals to slip through the boards. Of course, aesthetic choices can be made as well, and may include open-center or crossbuck designs, recognizable by the telltale "X" in the middle.

Yet most post-and-board fences look pretty similar until you study the methods used to join the two main components. There the similarities end, because there are a number of ways to construct a stable joint. The most common is probably to simply nail the boards to the outside faces of the post, butting them together at the joints. There are two caveats here, though, the first being not to let all the joints align if you can avoid it, and the second to consider the nature of the animals—if any—contained within.

The alignment problem can be solved by using 16' boards and spanning them over two 8' centers, staggering the middle joint so it falls midspan of the other two. The process just makes the individual bays all the more sturdy. The livestock present another problem, caused by their pushing against the fence boards, either to seek a better graze on the other side or to scratch their hides. Either way, if the creature is large enough, its weight may force the board fasteners right out of the posts. The solution is to mount the boards in the inside face of the posts if sizable stock is in the enclosure.

Other joint approaches include the application of 1 X 2 cleats to secure both sides of the on-edge rails, and the use of through mortises to house two rails side-by-side in the same socket. The latter requires the use of 6 X 6 posts on shorter centers to be effective.

The post tops can be left flat, cut at an angle to shed water (though the practice does expose more surface area of vulnerable end-grain to the elements), or covered with a flat or slanted 1 X 6 cap rail.

THE ZIGZAG RAIL FENCE

The zigzag, or worm fence as it was once called, is the ubiquitous split-rail barrier that defined America through its earliest period. Though it's excessive in its use of timber and takes up quite a bit of space on the ground, it remains popular as a holdover from our Colonial days.

Worm fencing is one of the few styles to require no posts, which may have been part of its attraction. Rather, long, riven rails are stacked upon one another and given support by the arrangement of the rows, which join each other at a 30-degree angle. Because the rails are split in a triangular fashion and the courses alternate from each run, the fence is reasonably stable. Zigzag fences are not usually built to great heights, 2' to 3' being common—though much taller examples exist.

The rails range from 8' to 11' in length and are split from cedar, though locust, larch, and sometimes yellow pine are also used. To postpone decay, the bottommost rails are set on rocks which keeps them slightly off the ground.

Originally, no fasteners were used to hold the rails together, owing to the fact that nails were so dear. That's not an issue today, so if any concerns about stability exist, the rails can be fastened to each other with 6" nails or gutter spikes. The angles can also be secured laterally using 4' lengths of $\frac{1}{2}$" reinforcing bar driven vertically into the ground on either side of the joints, so they're flush with the top rails.

It's interesting to note that 100-year-old specimens of worm fence still exist, and some demonstrate the ingenuity of our forebears in placing the smallest-diameter rails to the bottom of the stack to prevent small livestock such as poultry from getting past.

THE POST-AND-RAIL FENCE

Post-and-rail fencing includes the manufactured mortised-post and tapered-rail type sold at home and outdoor centers, and the double-post, stacked-rail style sometimes referred to as the Kentucky fence. It also encompasses large-timber mortised post-and-rail treatments and the Western jackleg or "buck" fence, which uses X-braced, aboveground posts.

The tapered-rail styles are often made of cedar, pine, and redwood, and come ready to go, with premortised 6' posts and precut 5" or 6" rails anywhere from 6' to 11' in length. Some manufacturers use round tenons rather than tapered ends on the rails and bore the mortises to suit. Once the posts are set, the fence stands 3-½' to 4' in height.

The double-post style is more rustic and universal, each post unit actually consisting of two posts, often smaller in diameter than a single post would be. The rails of each bay are alternately stacked where they join, then the tops of the posts are wrapped in rope or wire or held with wooden braces to keep the posts stable and secure. The fence usually stands between 4' and 5' tall, with bays at whatever length is convenient for the materials at hand. Many variations of the double-post style exist throughout the world, including examples that combine zigzag and double-post characteristics, and those that stack the rails to taper at one end.

Timber fences made of 6 X 6s or railroad ties make good road and driveway borders, and are usually lower to the ground, with only one or two rails being used. The mortises are cut into the sides of each post to a depth of 1" or 1-½", and the rails then fastened with large spikes. Posts can be 6'

in length, or shorter if only one rail is needed. Bays range from 6' to 8' in length.

The jackleg fence is an interesting deviation that may have enjoyed a resurrection in the American West. Six-foot poles 6" to 8" in diameter are crossed and joined at a 45-degree angle using shallow-cut notches and 6" nails. These buck posts are spaced every 10' and connected with 4" rails at the top of the cross and at two levels beneath it on either side. The rails are spiked to the buck posts, and sometimes connected at the ends in a half-lap joint. One benefit of the jackleg is that the posts don't need to be buried.

THE WIRE FENCE

Wire fencing of any kind is different from other types of fence in that there are often no rails involved—only bracing at the corners. With the exception of welded-wire mesh or poultry netting that you'd apply over an existing fence to contain animals or toddlers, the wire strand or fabric becomes the rails of the fence.

For this reason, the posts must be sturdy and set deeply. They also need to be pressure treated, or selected for their decay resistance. Posts 7' or 8' in length and at least 4" in diameter are required; for large livestock, diameters twice that are not uncommon.

Corner bays are beefed up by shortening them to half of the normal bay span and cutting notched mortises into the sides to support wooden-rail braces that stretch from the top of the terminal post to the bottom of the adjacent post. Sometimes upper and lower rails are utilized as well. Normal post spacing is set at 12' to 14' for barbed wire and 16' for woven wire. To protect the tops of the posts against

moisture absorption, they can be capped with galvanized or aluminum sheet tacked down at the sides.

To stretch the wire, one full wrap of material should be made around the end post before stapling. Then, only when that's secured, should the wire be unrolled and tightened in preparation for mounting. Fence-stretching is a several-person job and can be hazardous if done carelessly. Leather gloves should always be worn, and a vehicle or tractor should never be used to pull the wire directly because it may snap.

Instead, a puller bar or steel pipe is woven between the filler wires of the panel and pulled against a stay with cables mounted 6" from the top and bottom and attached to a pair of stretchers or come-alongs. These devices are, in turn, secured to a parked vehicle or a dummy post fixed beyond the terminal post at the run's opposite end. The ratchets on the stretching device tighten the wire with much more control than any vehicle could have. Once both end posts mountings are secured, the line post wire can be stapled every 6" or so, and the puller and remaining wire cut from the last post.

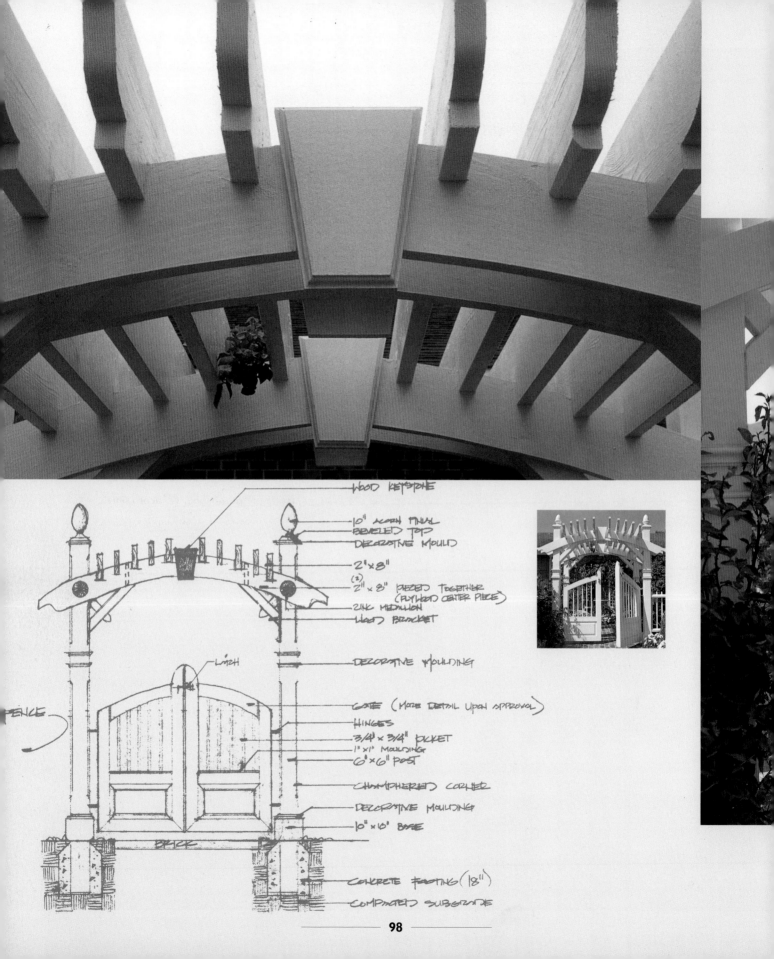

WOOD KEYSTONE

10" ACORN FINIAL
BEVELED TOP
DECORATIVE MOULD

2" x 8"

(2)
2" x 8" PIECED TOGETHER
(PLYWOOD CENTER PIECE)

ZINC MEDALLION
WOOD BRACKET

DECORATIVE MOULDING

GATE (MORE DETAIL UPON APPROVAL)

HINGES

3/4" x 3/4" PICKET

1" x 1" MOULDING

6" x 6" POST

CHAMPHERED CORNER

DECORATIVE MOULDING

10" x 10" BASE

LATCH

FENCE

BRICK

CONCRETE FOOTING (18")

COMPACTED SUBGRADE

The
Perfect Arbor

Those who need proof of the value of planning need look no further than the arbor and fence which distinguish the entrance to this residence in Greenville, South Carolina. Designed by the J. Dabney Peeples Design Associates in Easley, South Carolina and constructed on site by the client, the structure shows just what can be accomplished with dedicated forethought.

The plan views reveal that no single element is particularly elaborate; in fact, each component in both the arbor and the adjoining fence—save for the architectural specialties such as the finials and medallions—is standard lumberyard stock.

What makes these structures special is how they work together. For example, the arbor's ten-foot columns are simply straight 6 X 6s, yet they're transformed entirely with the addition of built-up 10" X 10" base panels trimmed in plinth molding, 10" acorn finials at the top, and chamfered edges cut between judiciously mounted center and upper moldings.

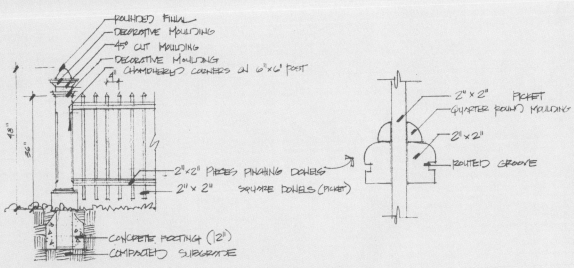

ROUNDED FINIAL
DECORATIVE MOULDING
45° CUT MOULDING
DECORATIVE MOULDING
¼" CHAMFERED CORNERS ON 6"×6" POST

48"

56"

2"×2" PICKET
QUARTER ROUND MOULDING
2"×2"
ROUTED GROOVE

2"×2" PIECES PINCHING DOWELS
2"×2" SQUARE DOWELS (PICKET)

CONCRETE FOOTING (12")
COMPACTED SUBGRADE

1/2 WOOD FENCE DETAIL

FENCE SHALL BE PAINTED WHITE   SCALE: 3/4"=1'—0"

The arches span 8-½', yet are not cut from a solid piece of wood. Rather, they are pieced together from 2 X 12s, which offer a broad enough surface to accommodate the required curve. A cut and routed wooden keystone conceals the joint of each arch. Brackets, each built up from triple layers of stock, connect the arches and the columns. Ten 2 X 8s on 6" centers serve as open rafters between the four arched elements.

The gate is fully framed and match paired, hung on lag-and-eye hinges. The stile cores are 42" 2 X 6s housed front and back in full-dimension lumber ripped to reveal the core edges; the latch stiles are 56" in height and similarly constructed, with radiused tops. Raised kick panels and 3/4" square pickets invoke just enough formality to correlate the arbor.

It is surrounded by a fence which carries similar elements of design, including square-dowel pickets on 4" centers and posts embellished in the manner of the pergola columns. The fence rails are 2 X 4s ripped and mounted between the posts to house the square pickets. Quarter-round moldings and a routed edge and groove enhance the appearance of the finished assembly.

A GATE

The gate—what it says and how it says it—is every bit as important as the fence itself. Keep in mind that this seemingly extra feature is not only likely to be highly visible, but will also be the one part of your fence that visitors to your residence will actually touch and come in contact with.

Most believe that a gate must reflect the design and style of the fence around it. Not entirely true. In fact, there are three approaches possible when considering what to put between the anchor posts of a new-built fence.

The first parallels conventional wisdom—that the gate and fence should be as one, different only in the fact that the gate has hinges and a latch. The match may be perfect in every detail, in which case the gate will effectively blend with (and maybe get lost in) the fence. Mounting the structure flush with the fence's surface serves to further conceal its presence, if that's your goal. A design such as this might reflect a need for consistency, or express a desire for privacy in its discreetness.

Left: Firehouse gate, 1803.
Above: The gate stands out from the living fence made by the hedge.

The second approach is exactly the opposite. When the gate contrasts with the fence, it stands up and gets noticed. This can be accomplished in any number of ways, from using an entirely different medium (such as wrought iron) for the gate, to using similar materials in a different size or pattern. Whatever the method, this treatment stops the flow and continuity of the fence line and announces the gate's presence in an obvious way.

The third treatment is a combination of the first two. The gate can be integrated with the fence it's attached to, but may have distinguishing characteristics placed to catch the eye. These might include some design changes or a specific pattern. This approach allows the continuity of the fence to remain unscathed while bringing the desired degree of attention to the gate itself.

Above, left: The pattern of the gate mirrors that of the arch and the door behind it.

Above, center: The gate is discreet and inconspicuous within this tall board fence.

Above, right: This gateway has an arch across the span, and the gate top is bowed to mimic the curve. The infill tries to mirror that on the porch railing.

Right: Just a suggestion of a gate in this picket fence line.

Left: The gate components are made of a different material than the fence and arbor, but complement it easily.

The arch and the gate employ reverse curves.

PLANNING THE GATE

The task of planning is not as simple as it might appear, nor is it something that should be done after the fence is completed. There are a number of things to think about when planning a gate, and most involve the placement of the fence itself.

Placement: Gates are rarely just decorative. As nice as they might look, they have a purpose—to permit access somewhere along the fence line to an area enclosed within or outside of the fence. This access may fall conveniently at a place where there's a break in a hedge line or a natural feature in the landscape that invites a gate. Placement can also be dictated by the presence of a path or walkway in the general landscape plan.

Even without a formal blueprint, you can use common sense to establish where a gate should go. Existing foot traffic patterns are good guidelines in placing a gate, and consideration of future plans—a playground, new gardens, or structural

additions, for example—can prevent difficulties later on. Obviously, natural barriers such as large trees or rock outcroppings immediately establish where not to place a gate.

Size: This is a matter of design and function. If practical concerns didn't matter, the span and height of the gate would simply be determined by the height of the fence and the width of the path it accommodated. But things larger than people often must pass through gates. Lawnmowers, yard furniture, wheelbarrows, and other bulky items require an opening that's convenient to both you and them.

If the gate closes across a driveway, there are other things to consider. Gateposts must be substantially stronger and deeper to support the wider structure. The hinge and latch hardware must be stouter. And width shouldn't be established by your vehicle alone, especially if the gate is in a curve. Large cars and service trucks need more clearance than you might think to maneuver safely.

Gate openings wider than 8' or so could benefit from a double-gate design, which reduces the strain on a single post

Above: The large driveway gate is heavy and imposing, and would be a small feat of engineering to complete in wood. The owner chose instead to cut an appropriate pattern into 1 X 8 boards, and mount them with carriage bolts to a pair of sturdy tubular-steel farm gates [below], which were then hung from the posts.

The gate swings into the corner

and usually offers a better appearance as well. With any wide gate, height and bracing is important, and that's discussed in detail later on in this chapter.

Swing: The direction in which the gate swings will depend on where it's located and to some extent the kind of post it's hung on. If the gate is situated as an entry to a place or a piece of property, it should swing inward. If it's located within the borders of a lot, it can swing in the direction of initial flow (an example would be a gate to a private garden tucked into the corner of a larger yard). And, if it's placed at or near the juncture of two perpendicular fence lines, it should swing against the corner so it's out of the way when standing open.

An exception would be in the case of a gate placed on a slope, where it's prudent to set its swing away from the uphill side to prevent it from interfering with the ground; when the gate posts run parallel to the slope, the swing should be toward the downhill side so the facing boards won't have to be cut square to clear the ground when the gate is fully opened.

At the top of a series of steps, safety dictates that a gate swing away from the steps so it has to be opened before one proceeds downward. In case you're wondering, gates aren't usually placed at the bottom of a flight of steps unless there's a landing, simply because it's awkward to lean over to manipulate the latch.

These guidelines notwithstanding, if the gate and the posts it lies between are the same dimension in thickness, the gate should be placed in line with the posts, and the hinges

The gate swings away from the landing, which provides a zone of safety before the steps begin.

mounted so the gate can swing in one or the other direction. Likewise, if the gate is matched to wider posts, it should be centered within the post shoulders and hinged appropriately. However, if it's aligned with one edge of the posts, it should swing open in that direction.

Because of the inevitable stresses that will be transferred to the post on which the gate hangs, the gatepost with the hinges should be the one that was specially anchored, as explained in Chapter Seven. If, when constructing the fence, you're undecided about the direction of swing, you can always deep-anchor both gateposts to permit you full design flexibility for later on.

DESIGNING THE GATE

A clear and well-thought plan is essential to the success of a gate. Estimating dimensions or trying to design as you go usually results in errors which are not always easy to correct afterwards. To minimize such problems, it's easy enough to put your plan down on paper, which will give you a chance to develop some visuals as well.

Begin by purchasing a small packet of graph or engineer's paper, the kind with the light blue squares, scaled at $\frac{1}{4}$" or $\frac{1}{2}$" apart. Then, using a pencil and ruler, sketch the gate-posts and a partial bay on either side of them, including all the visible elements. It's important that this drawing, rough as it is, be to scale, so on an 8-$\frac{1}{2}$" X 11" sheet, for example, one inch can equal one foot and still leave a comfortable border. If you need a larger surface, it's simple enough to tape several sheets together with the squares aligned.

The idea is to experiment with different looks while still making each design fit in the space prescribed. Since you'll be working over and over with the same basic template, you can either photocopy the original to create an ample supply of base drawings (be forewarned that the blue guide lines will not copy particularly well), or use tracing paper as an overlay, which you can replace with each new sketch. Either way, the exercise will provide you with an accurate picture that you can easily change to suit your taste.

BUILDING THE GATE

Though you can use other elements to embellish any gate you build, wood is the essence of its construction. Like the fence, a gate's framework should be solid and well joined, but even more effectively so, because it's subject to stresses that the fence doesn't see. Swinging, banging, children hanging—it's all part of the gate's life, and a severe one at that.

Unless there's a good reason to choose otherwise, it's best to use the same kind of lumber for the gate as for the fence. Some exceptions might include beefing up the gate framing with larger-dimension wood if needed, or using a more stable species for strength if you think it's required.

Whatever wood you use, the construction will remain the same: there'll be a solid frame, braced in some way against

Above: The gate breaks just enough from thefence to make it interesting.

Below: A perimeter-frame gate with board infill and masive forged hinges.

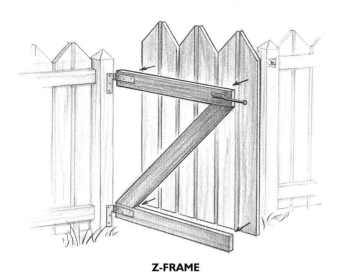

Z-FRAME

PERIMETER FRAME

sagging, to which there will be attached a facing or infill of covering material. Hinges fastened to one stile will support the gate, and a latch secured to the opposite stile will hold it shut until someone comes to open it.

Essentially, there are two common methods used in building the frame. The first approach is called is the Z-frame, a simple arrangement in which the framing boards are laid flat to join each other on edge, the brace stretching diagonally from the top of the latch side to the bottom of the hinge side to form a "Z" figure. The second method is the perimeter frame, in which the framing members are set against the infill on edge to make a sturdy box that's braced internally with a similar diagonal.

Though the frame design of the fence will dictate to some degree the design of the gate, the frames do not necessarily have to match. If, for whatever reason, you need a sturdy boxed gate but have a fence with the stringers on edge, the two can be matched inconspicuously by using hinges that allow the gate to hang in alignment with the posts. Other considerations that might guide your choice are noted in the next two examples.

THE Z-FRAME

■ The "Z" is considered easier to construct because there are fewer components involved. Only two joints need to be assembled.

■ The Z-frame is not as structurally rigid as the perimeter type because it lacks its own dedicated stiles. The infill, or siding, needs to provide much of the support for the frame, so it too must be substantial enough to withstand the rigors of constant use.

■ Additional strength can be borrowed by utilizing let-in joints at the corners, or reinforcing them on the surface with galvanized corner braces.

■ The "Z" pattern does not have to be limited to use with the framing members on edge. They can be turned flat and the joints rabbeted before fastening. This allows more freedom in making the gate consistent with the fence construction.

■ Z-framed gates cannot house an inset fill. The infill must be nailed onto the surface of the frame, whether it's used flat or on edge.

THE PERIMETER FRAME

■ Perimeter-framed gates are slightly more difficult to construct because there are more pieces to it, and six, rather than two joints, involved. All five members must be measured to fit squarely.

■ The perimeter frame is self-supporting. It will function as a gate even without the infill attached.

■ Rabbeted or half-lapped joints and metal corner braces

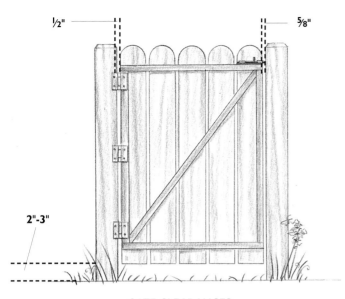

GATE CLEARANCES

can be used to provide further strength at the corners.

■ The framing members can be installed flat or on edge. When used on edge, it's preferable to use a shouldered joint as opposed to a simple butt joint.

■ The flat-oriented perimeter frame can support an inset infill. The infill (lattice, tongue-and-groove boards, or precut panel) is secured between nailer strips on the frame's inner ace, and the diagonal brace is set flat or ripped to the thickness required to fit flush with the edge.

Once you've settled on a frame design, you can begin construction. But don't put a saw to wood before you take some exact measurements and record them on paper so there'll be no confusion over what the correct dimensions are. You've done this once already, of course, to rough-in the gate, but it won't hurt to double-check your work to $\frac{1}{4}$" tolerances.

Measure the height of the gateposts and the distance between them at points 6" from the top and bottom of each post. Use a level to check that the inside faces of the posts are plumb and parallel (you can lay the level horizontally across the faces to see the degree of distortion); if they're not, you'll have to make adjustments in the frame to compensate. Typical clearances between the hinge post and stile are from $\frac{1}{4}$" to $\frac{1}{2}$", and between the latch stile and post, from $\frac{1}{2}$" to $\frac{5}{8}$". The more refined the gate, the closer the

spacing should be. A rustic gate can manage easily with tolerances greater than these.

That done, stretch and level a line across the front of the posts about 2" from the ground. Measure down from this line to establish the degree of slope, if any, that might exist between each post, and note it on your drawing. If it's conspicuous enough, you'll need to cut the gate siding to follow the angle of the slope.

The hardware you choose and your arrangement of the gate stop may also affect the finished dimensions of the gate. As explained in Chapter Six, hinges can be surface-mounted or mortised, or hung from lag screw hooks, and each method has different clearance requirements. Too, the latch mechanism you settle on might require that you make some adjustments or cut a mortise to allow for clearance.

Gate stops can be often be eliminated by letting the latch serve as the stop, but a finished gate will have a true stop if only to indicate the direction of swing. If the gate is designed and hinged to swing both ways, then no stop should be used.

The most substantial stop is a vertical strip of wood fastened to the latch post. It can be a piece of 1 X 2 or 2 X 2, cut the full height of the gate and secured with No. 8 decking screws. Unfortunately, it's also the most obtrusive because it extends from the face of the post. A similar arrangement—with a similar complication—has the stop fastened to the rear of the post.

It's possible, as another option, to allow the siding on the gate to serve as the stop. In order to do this, the siding boards must be arranged so the final piece on the latch side extends beyond the frame by 1-$\frac{1}{2}$" or so. Conversely, if the gatepost siding board on the fence is arranged in this manner, it can become the stop. In both cases, the adjacent boards on the neighboring member must follow the spacing pattern so no drastic gaps occur between the fence and the gate.

Once you're ready to build, cut the frame components to length. On both types of frame, the horizontal parts should overlay the vertical pieces to protect the uprights' end grain from water. Now is the time to plan and cut any rabbets or half- laps if you're going to include those joints in your plan.

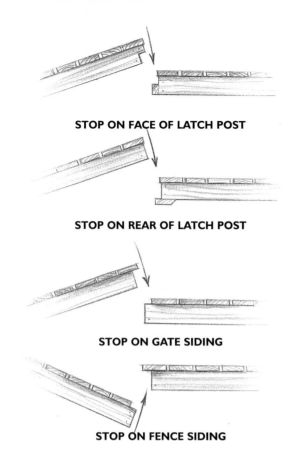

STOP ON FACE OF LATCH POST

STOP ON REAR OF LATCH POST

STOP ON GATE SIDING

STOP ON FENCE SIDING

Lay the pieces on a flat surface such as a workbench or garage floor, and true them up using a tape measure, and a framing square on the perimeter style. Check for square on both perimeter and "Z" styles by comparing diagonal measurements, taken from the outside corners of the crossmembers. (They should be within $\frac{3}{16}$" of each other.)

Do not use nails to fasten the joints. For the strongest, longest-lasting connections, bond the joints with an exterior construction adhesive and connect them with No. 10 X 3" decking screws—at least two per joint.

Check again for square, then place the completed frame over the diagonal member you plan to use. Make certain that the diagonal extends from the lower hinge corner to the upper latch corner, or it will not support the gate in compression as it's supposed to. Using a sharp pencil, mark the cut lines onto the brace, then cut outside the lines. Tap the brace into position, and fasten it by driving No. 10 screws from the sides and through the vertical members.

If you plan on using a wire turnbuckle brace, it must be oriented in just the opposite direction to the solid brace. That's because it works in tension, not compression, and must

A pegged mortise-and-tenon corner joint.

hang from the upper hinge corner.

At this point, you can add the infill as needed. Lay the finished frame back down, with the infill side facing up. Cut the boards to size and lay them vertically (or diagonally or horizontally, if that's the case) over the frame, beginning your alignment with the hinge-side stile. Test-place all the boards before nailing them to avoid any surprises. Minor adjustments can be made by "stretching" the infill by spacing the boards slightly, or narrowing it by trimming or planing the edge of the last board or two. Fasten the infill by the same means as you installed the fence boards.

Next, measure and mark the hinge positions and drill pilot holes for the screw fasteners using a bit about $\frac{1}{3}$ the size of the screw diameter. If the hinges are to be mortised, do it now. Fasten the hinge leaves to the gate using screws just short enough to avoid penetrating the opposite face of the wood.

To hang the gate, prop it up on blocks and check the clearances at the posts. Given that everything fits, mark the hinge leaf and screw-hole outlines on the hinge post and drill the holes. If there are indications of binding, you'll need to trim the gate at the latch stile to alleviate the problem. Then fasten the hinges to the post with long screws of the appropriate diameter.

Measure and mark the latch position along with its catch, and mount the hardware on the gate and post. If you haven't already installed the gate stop, do it before fastening the hardware so there will be no question as to the alignment of the latch.

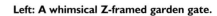
Left: A whimsical Z-framed garden gate.

Below: This self-closing gate uses a chain and weight in lieu of a latch.

the hand-crafted gate

I t's often the indigenous materials that work best in a special situation, and this driveway gate is a perfect case in point. Designed and built for the Rose Cottages in the mountain community of Hendersonville, North Carolina by Charles Stafford, a local landscape designer, the gate represents an exemplary use of materials at hand.

Examine it closely and you'll see that each 5' X 6' frame—consisting of the hinge and latch stiles, a sill board, and three rails—is made up of dimensional 2 X 4s, routed and fastened face-to-edge. Between the stiles, 22 rough-sawn fillers measuring $7/8$" X 2-$3/4$" are evenly spaced 3" on center. They too are fastened to each of the three rails and to the sill from below. 1X4 face boards cover the rails and all wooden members were stained and water-sealed with an exterior clear wood finish. The open spacing allows the frames to be light-weight enough that the center rail and paired screw joints are sufficient to keep the gates from sagging.

The contoured tops of each gate are edged with ½" soft copper tubing, dressed in patina and fastened through predrilled holes with 1-¼" tacks. On the face of the gate, found-wood honeysuckle branches are tacked down in a natural fan pattern from the corners, and twigs created using ¼" copper tubing, likewise predrilled and tacked in place.

The 5" leaves were cut individually into oval shapes and sanded at the edges to blunt the sharp corners. A Dremel rotary grinder cut the veins into each leaf. Before tacking the leaves between slats adjoining the twigs and branches, the wood was given a dark stain and sealed from the elements.

The design is adaptable for width and would work just as well for a garden entry gate by narrowing it to suit.

A TYPICAL PROJECT

Judging from its popularity alone, it probably wouldn't be incorrect to assume that the neighborhood fence of choice is one variation or another on the picket style. So what could be more appropriate than a pictorial chapter on the step-by-step construction of a properly built front yard picket fence?

The example shown in the next few pages was erected to enclose a 32' X 60' yard—136 running feet all told, including a short return at the rear. The builder, Jonathan Clarke of Fairview, North Carolina, specializes in restoration and period carpentry, and for the most part built the fence on site

from detailed planning sketches worked out beforehand. Even with such meticulous preparation, Clarke acknowledges that he had to make minor adjustments as he went along: "It is woodworking, after all, and wood is not a stable medium." Besides, even a craftsman has to expect some variation in 136 feet of work running over natural terrain.

The owner wanted an architecturally appropriate structure tall enough to discourage trespassing, but not so intimidating so as to be unwelcoming to visitors. Clarke came to common ground by incorporating a pleasant concave dip into the picket line of each bay, repeating the pattern in natural

LIST OF MATERIALS

rhythm through the length of the fence—save for the front gate, which reverses the pattern with a convex crown. A side gate is built discreetly into one bay with the addition of a center post, leaving the pattern relatively intact.

For longevity and the ready availability of materials, the fence was constructed of pressure-treated Southern yellow pine, standard lumberyard fare in that part of the country. You can see, from the materials list at right, that only three sizes of dimensional lumber were needed to complete the entire project, which—with occasional maintenance and a protective coating of paint—can be expected to last at least 40 years.

1

Having the benefit of a level lot simplifies the construction procedure significantly. On this project, it was possible to cut the post finials and all the stringer dadoes beforehand, using the plan to transfer the scaled dimensions to actual size. After establishing a base point for the four-faced finial, the upper and lower shoulders are measured, at 13" and 16-½", for the top stringers, followed by those for the bottom stringers at 52" and 55-½".

2

Here, a sliding bevel is used to mark the dado notch's shoulder lines. If the stringers are perfectly level, a combination square would work as well.

3

A marking gauge, being used to scribe a line to indicate the dado's depth of cut.

4

Cutting a series of saw kerfs beforehand assists in completing the dadoes. The circular saw is set to the proper depth and, after first making the shoulder cuts, several parallel passes are made through the post.

5

A mallet and mortise chisel are used to remove waste from the dado cut. This is the notch for the top stringer on the short center post, destined for the side gate.

6

The guidelines for the finial cuts are marked on the post, using the blade of a combination square.

7

A handsaw makes quick and accurate cuts to remove corner waste and complete the finials.

8

Here, top and bottom stringer lines have been set according to the plan specifications, and fastened between corner posts already plumbed and set in place. The fence post locations have been marked on 8' centers, and the two gate post positions are 4' apart. All postholes are excavated to a 3' depth.

9

The full-length posts are first set on a bed of several inches of compacted crushed stone. Then final height is established by measuring the distance between the lower shoulder of the dado and the stringer line, then cutting that amount from the bottom of the post.

10

Once the stringer line is level and even with the dado shoulder, the post is plumbed using a level.

11

Earth fill is packed around the post to secure it in the hole. A tool handle or a length of 2 X 2 makes a good soil tamper.

12

A completed leg of fence-line posts, with the stringer lines removed. The two in the foreground are the gate posts, which were furnished with anchor cleats to help stabilize them.

13

The blade of a sliding bevel being used to check the plumb of a post and the end cut after one stringer has been

installed. Note that the end of the stringer falls directly at the midpoint of the post dado.

14

The sliding bevel marks the end cut for the adjoining stringer. The opposite end of this stringer will be cut after establishing the exact distance between the midpoint of the post shown and that of the next post down the line. On paper, that dimension is a constant; in the real world (even the carefully measured one), it can vary by $\frac{1}{2}$" or more.

15

The abutting ends of two well-joined stringers show hardly a gap between the components, and the faces of both the post and stringers are flush.

16

The corner posts use 1-½"-square by 3-½" notches to house the stringers where they change direction. These mortises are marked with a gauge and cut exclusively with a chisel.

17

The 1 X 4 pickets are precut according to the scaled plan, mostly from 10' and 12' hand-picked lumberyard stock. Because of minor variations, each bay is measured and the spacing adjusted to suit. The space between pickets, bay to bay, can range between 2-¾" and 3" without being conspicuous, as long as spacing within each individual bay is consistent. Here, the first picket is clamped in place after measuring for height and position, and plumbed with a level.

18

With upper and lower ends clamped, the mounting holes can be drilled. One fastener per joint is all that's needed for the first stage.

19

The next picket is positioned for height, checked for spacing, plumbed, and prepared for fastening with the drilling of a pilot hole.

20

Subsequent pickets are installed in the same manner, each being plumbed as shown before final fastening. One half of the bay is completed before starting on the other.

21

The procedure is repeated on the second side. Accurate measurement of height is critical from the start, both for consistency and to assure that the concave arc remains balanced within its bay.

22

The initial picket is clamped and plumbed prior to drilling. If minor inaccuracies exist in length, the difference can be taken from the bottom, where it's least visible. An obviously short picket will have to be replaced, and may be able to be utilized at another location.

23

The final mounting hole for this series is completed. In softwood, the pilot drill can be one-third to one-half the-diameter of the intended screw shank; a countersink bit isn't needed because the design of the screw allows the head to sink itself.

24

Each picket is now fastened with two screws per joint, spaced approximately 2" apart. The screws used on this project are square-drive rather than Phillips type.

25

One bay completed. This pattern will serve as the model to which the remaining bays must be compared. Picket spacing and the consistency of the arc from one bay to the next is critical.

26

The front gate, hung from two butt hinges. The Z-frame design is simple and lightweight and not so conspicuous behind the crowned picket infill.

27

The back side of the through latch reveals how it operates. The thumb lever is of sufficient length to accommodate gate thicknesses up to 2-¾".

28

A modified butt hinge used on the side gate. The gate leaf's oblong shape is the reason the hinge is termed "modi-

fied," for it is not quite a T-hinge. The screws that came with this hardware happened to be sufficient to support the gate; they are 1-¼" in length.

29

True to its intent, the side gate gets lost in the rhythm of the pickets. The latch post at center is purposely made short to keep it unobtrusive; it must be there to support the latch.

30

The completed fence (p. 116) demonstrates how pleasant the contoured pickets pattern can be. The yard, is now private, yet still inviting and accessible.

Fences are made in a great variety of styles, using indigenous materials of every description. In the pages that follow, there are examples of historic and contemporary fences from all over the United States, and a number from other countries besides. In analyzing the structure and details carefully, it becomes apparent that the fences of America borrowed heavily from the experience of those that came from other places. It's also obvious that much of the American fence has its roots firmly planted in a rural and agricultural past.

Split rails housed in split and mortised posts on a ranch that stretches to the sea near Yatchats, Oregon.

Right: Wood from nearby Norway spruce forests is plentiful and therefore used almost profligately here on an Austrian farm near Salzburg. It serves to keep the farm cattle out of the neat and tidy yard and garden around the mountain home. A minimum of digging is needed in this stony soil with this cross-brace post arrangement.

Opposite: An unusual stake-and-rider fence on a Montana ranch. Far enough from the Rockies that wood is not abundant, it economizes on that material and uses barbed wire strung along the rider. The smaller-diamter rider is inserted through a hole drilled in the stake.

Above: The large cattle ranches employing paniolos, or cowboys, on the Big Island in Hawaii requires sturdy fences for the large beef animals. Here a gnarled rail fence of the ohi 'a tree create something not only effective , but splendidly scenic.

Left: Snow fence, or "drift" fence, is identical to fencing used to control blowing sand. A 4'-tall fence of 50-percent porosity (gauged by the spacing between the wooden slats) can collect nearly three cubic yards of sand per running foot.

Below: Lattice panel inset beneath an arch, between two extended posts. The use of lattice opens up the top of an otherwise solid panel fence; the arch breaks the plane for a gate, or for an occasional respite in an especially long run.

Right: A picket fence of pressure-treated pine, with routed posts and cut finials. The pickets are stacked and cut in groups to keep the shape of the spades and the inside radii consistent.

Left, above and below: Double gates provide full access to a wide path and, from a practical standpoint, aid in moving furniture and bulky items. The gates on the lower left demonstrate the use of a perimeter gate frame; the ones at left are constructed with Z-frames.

Below, right: A slant-top picket style, with closely-spaced pickets. This fence was built to keep roaming animals from the yard and gardens; nonetheless, with the gap between pickets less than one-quarter the width of the pickets themselves, the fence presents a blurred, almost solid surface from a distance. Opening the spaces would make the fence more neighbor-friendly. Exposed hinges and the shadow of the cross-brace at the center is the only indication of a gate within the fence line.

Above, left: A well-plotted pasture fence line.

Above, right: To the dismay of the pressure-treated lumber industry, vinyl has found a niche in fence-building. Formerly just for lattice and looks, prefabricated vinyl fencing is now functional and attractive, and comes in a variety of traditional fence styles.

Above, left: A stepped-frame fence set on a fairly steep slope. This example uses triple stringers on edge and vertical infill board, inset within the individual frames.

Above, right: A three-rail post-and-board fence in a grazing pasture. The boards are fastened to the inside face of the posts so horses within the enclosure won't be successful in pushing the boards from their nail sockets.

Opposite, above: **A post-and-board pattern with cross-buck rails and center stiles. This is a strong, attractive fence with an open design. It requires a considerable amount of lumber to construct.**

Opposite, below: **Sometimes a simple treatment can put the perfect finish on a good design. This curved-top gate was built to fit the brick column opening, then embellished with a pair of antique strap hinges, forged in Portugal over 100 years ago.**

Above: **Sheet-metal caps prevent water from settling in the end grain of the posts in this barbed-wire pasture fence.**

Below: **A three-rail split-cedar fence encloses a small horse pasture. Adjoining rails are fit halfway into the post mortises; post layout is critical with this design, and each bay must be set and assembled before moving on to the next.**

Above: Post-and-board fence typifies 20th-century rural America as much as worm fencing did in the years before. The triple-piece fan gate braces are attractive and yet still functional.

Left: The two-rail style is economical and traverses hills and dips comfortably. Note the use of locust posts with painted white pine boards.

Opposite page: : Post-and-board fence in Carolina horse country.

Above: Split-rail zigzag fence protects an old homestead.

Opposite, right: A very rustic random-picket fence in a country setting. These pickets were likely riven, or split, and then hand hewn.

This fence near Kyoto is hardly useful for keeping anything in or out of a piece of land, but is a property boundary marker of legal and ceremonial significance. In Japan bamboo seems to pervade all aspects of life, from household materials to ceremonial objects.

BAMBOO FENCING

Bamboo is one of the most versatile and useful plants known to humans. Of the world's grasses, it is the largest and most magnificent. It has been documented to grow as much as 3 feet in 24 hours. It has one columnular shape, but many sizes up to perhaps 12 inches in diameter and 100 feet high. It is hollow, and divided longitudinally by walled nodes

A woven split bamboo fence near Bumthang, in the kingdom of Bhutan, keeps chickens and straying cattle out of the farm garden. The fence, like the fortress monastery in the background, provides an air of stability and strength.

so that it is stiff and strong, yet light. It is these qualities that make it useful as fencing material, both for posts and for horizontal rails or bars. Unfortunately, it is not durable in contact with the ground, so that posts decay quite rapidly. Nonetheless, thousands of fences of bamboo occur throughout tropical and sub-tropical landscapes.

A split rail fence of American chestnut wends its way over the landscape near Cooperstown, New York. The species was once widely distributed in New England and was an extremely durable, beautiful, and easily split wood. A blight from Europe largely wiped out chestnut throughout the United States, and we lost one of the world's best natural fencing materials.

ACKNOWLEDGEMENTS

ADDITIONAL PHOTOGRAPHY

Special thanks to Lawrence S. Hamilton of Islands and Highlands Environmental Consultancy in Charlotte, Vermont for the photographs on pages 15 (top left), 91 (bottom), 95 (top),124-125, 126, 127 (top), 138, 139, and 140-41, and for his years of effort in recording fences and gates of the world. And to Gregory K. Dreicer, Curator, National Building Museum, Washington DC, for his support with the exhibit "Between Fences". Thanks, too, to Anita G. Mannon and Environmentally Sensitive Logging & Lumber Co., Inc., of Copper Hill, Virginia who so generously provided the photograph on page 47. Thanks, as well, to the Rainforest Alliance (65 Bleeker St., New York, NY 10012), for their generosity in providing the logo of their Smart Wood Program, which appears on page 47. And thanks to Raymond Emery of Emery Fence Company in Travelers Rest, South Carolina for providing the photograph at the bottom of page 37. We would also like to thank and credit the following people for contributing to this work: Evan Bracken, for the photographs on pages 8, 9 (center), and 113 (top); Dana Irwin for the photographs on pages 14 (top), 46 (top), 95 (center), 127 (bottom), 134 (bottom), and 135; David Jenkins for the photographs on pages 6, 46 (left), 97, 134 (top), 136, and 137; and the author, for the photographs on pages 37 (top), 42 (bottom), 45, 46 (bottom), 78, 94, 96, 129 (top), and 133.

SPECIAL PHOTOGRAPHS

We would like to acknowledge The Library of Congress for the following photographs: page 12, "Fence Built in 1890, Ola, Idaho", photograph by Dorothea Lange, Library of Congress, Prints and Photographs Division, FSA-OWI Collection, LC-USF34-21606-C; page 15 (upper right), "Farm House of Fred Coalter, Grundy County, Iowa, April 1940", photograph by John Vachon, Library of Congress, Prints and Photographs Division, FSA-OWI Collection, USF33-1805; page 16 (lower left), "Sunday Afternoon at Home, Alexandria, Virginia, June 1943", photograph by Ann Rosener, Library of Congress, Prints and Photographs Division, FSA-OWI Collection. The photographs on page 14 (lower left) "Glidden Steel Barb Wire", and page 15 (center) "Ellwood Steel Fences" are from the collection of the Ellwood House Association and Museum in DeKalb, Illinois.

LOCATION PHOTOGRAPHY

Particular thanks to the staff at J. Dabney Peeples Design Associates of 222 Zion Church Road, Easley, SC 29640 for so courteously sharing their time and expertise in arranging location photograpy. And special thanks to the McCalley family of Greenville, South Carolina, for so generously opening their home and gardens to us for the book cover and related photographs within. And, of course, many thanks to the fence owners who contributed so richly to this book:

Randy and Jacque Bell
David and Deborah Lichtenfelt
Riley Owens
Jim Tomlin
Keith Holtermann
Marsha Kelso of Rose Cottages
Leona Farquhar of The Merry Miller
Jeffrey and Alicia Boyle
Ernest Park
Charles Fisher
John and Katie Strickland
Charlie and Judy Brown

Alice and David Kraebber
Bobbi Sommer
Jennifer and Jeremy Wainwright of The Pine Crest Inn
Greg Bounds of The Scarlett Inn
Howard Stafford of The White Gate Inn
Sheila Meadows
Joy K. Peterson
Roger Bean
Don Tomlinson
Lynn Cordell
Old Salem, Incorporated

GLOSSARY OF TERMS

Anchor. A length of wood or metal used at the base of a post to increase contact with the ground.

Anchor post. Any braced post used at a corner, end, or gate of a fence.

Auger. A post hole digger that cuts into the soil by clockwise rotation.

Barbed wire. Two strands of smooth wire twisted together around short, regularly spaced barbs.

Barbless cable. Two strands of smooth wire twisted together without barbs.

Batten. A filler board used to cover the joints on board fence infill.

Bay. One section of fence, from one post to the next, including stringers and infill.

Bevel. An angle cut into the face of the joining ends of a rail or board to provide a larger contact area for the joint so it's not conspicuous when it expands.

Board. The main component of a board fence, usually installed vertically, or horizontally in a pasture fence.

Brace. A horizontal or diagonal member used to support a post, consisting of wood, metal, or wire.

Buck fence. A wooden fence with no buried members, sometimes called a jackleg fence.

Butt joint. A basic wood joint in which the ends of rails or boards are simply aligned, placed together, and secured.

Cap. One or more boards fastened horizontally along the top rail or posts of a fence for rain protection or decoration.

Clamshell. A post hole digger that uses two semi-cylindrical scoops on hinges, each attached to a long handle.

Cleat. A short piece of wood used to support a rail or board and which serves as a nailer. Also the piece used to connect the tops of paired posts in a double-post and rail fence.

Collector. A fence designed to capture and contain drifting snow or sand.

Corner post. A vertical post at which a fence changes direction.

Cross fence. A fence set up between boundary or perimeter fence lines.

Dado. An open notch cut into a post to hold a rail.

Deadman. An anchor fastened to the bottom of a post, or an anchor placed several feet from a post to serve as a moor for a brace or guy wire.

Deflector. A fence designed to guide or divert wind or blowing snow.

Dog leg. A jog in a straight fence line.

End lap. A wood joint used to connect rails or boards in which the ends are cut to overlap one another.

End post. A vertical post located at an opening or gate.

End splice. The end of a wire tied off at an anchor post.

Fascia. A wide board fastened to the top of fence posts to shed rain and tie the fence together.

Field fence. Woven wire panel, manufactured with a variety of spacing dimensions.

Filler. The horizontal wires of a woven-wire fence, except for the top and bottom members.

Footing. The foundation of a fence post, consisting of the post hole, a stone bed, and filler material.

Galvanized. Covered with a zinc coating for protection against the weather. Used on wire, fasteners, and hardware.

Gauge. An industry standard assigned to indicate the thickness of wire; higher numbers indicate thinner wire and staple components. Screw fasteners use a different schedule, in which higher numbers represent thicker pieces.

H-Brace. The horizontal brace between two posts.

Heartwood. The wood from the center of a log, which is more resistant to decay than the surrounding sapwood.

High-tensile. A type of fence wire with extraordinary breaking strength.

Infill. The fence surface itself, which gets fastened to the framework of posts and stringers.

Jackleg. A type of fence that uses X-crossed braces rather than buried posts, and horizontal rails. Also called a buck fence.

Kentucky fence. Another name for the double-post and rail fence.

Level. To be even and parallel with the horizontal plane.

Line post. Any vertical fence post positioned between anchor posts.

Miter. An angle cut into the edge of the joining ends of a rail or board to increase the surface area of a corner joint.

Mortise. The channel or opening cut into a fence post for the purpose of holding a rail or other component.

Nailer. A strip of wood used to support another member and to nail against.

Panel fence. A fence or framed screen made from any variety of panel goods, which include plywood, lattice, hardboard, and glass.

Perimeter fence. A fence set up along property

lines or boundaries.

Picket. The shaped verticals that fasten to the rails of a picket fence and make up the infill.

Plumb. To be perfectly straight up-and-down, or on a vertical plane.

Post. A ground-anchored, vertical member of a wooden fence.

Post-and-board. A fence style used mostly in rural applications to enclose pasture, horses, and large livestock, and which consists of sturdy posts connected by two or three plank-type rails.

Post-and-rail. A type of fence that uses mortised posts and split, squared, or turned rails which are housed in the mortises. Also a variety of styles that include the double-post technique with rails between, and jackleg or X-braced arrangements.

Rail. A horizontal framing member of a fence, also called a stringer. Likewise, the horizontal framing of a gate.

Sapwood. The newer-growth wood outside the heartwood of a log, and less resistant to decay.

Shadow box. A vertical-board fence style that uses staggered pickets mounted to both sides of the rail.

Stay. The vertical wire in a woven wire fence.

Stile. A vertical framing member of a gate, to which either the hinges or a latch is fastened.

Stretcher. A braced line post.

Stringer. The horizontal rail of a fence.

Tamper. A heavy rod used to compact the soil around a fence post.

Terminal post. A vertical post at the end of a run of fence.

Toenail. A nailing method used to join perpendicular components that involves driving the nail at a 45-degree angle through the nailed, and into the solid, member.

Turnbuckle. An assembly consisting of two eyebolts and a threaded frame, used to tighten cables or rods that support a gate or wooden framework.

Twitch stick. A piece of wood used to tighten brace wires by twisting them together.

Wattle fence. A barrier made of slender branches, reeds, or withes woven between vertical posts.

Worm fence. A zigzag rail fence.

Woven fence. A variation of the wattle design in which lath or slats are woven between horizontal rails mounted to vertical posts.

Zigzag fence. A low fence consting of rails arranged so that each section is at an angle to the next for support.

INDEX